A CHILD'S WAR

A CHILD'S WAR

WORLD WAR II
THROUGH THE EYES OF CHILDREN

KATI DAVID

RYAN PUBLISHING
Independence and Quality

First published in Great Britain 1989.

British Library Cataloguing in Publication Data

David, Kati, *1935-*
    A Child's War.
    1. World War   2. Biographies collections
    I. Title
    940.54'8

    ISBN 1-870805-03-8

Ryan Publishing Co. Ltd.
16 Market Place, Peterborough, PE6 8EA.

Designed in Paris by Franck Marest.
Origination by Wenham Arts.
Printed in Scotland.

To the Unknown Child of past and present wars.

Contents

Acknowledgments

To those persons who shared their memories with me, and in particular the fifteen on whose true life experiences these stories are based. Without their confidence and their willingness to share their personal memories and most intimate feelings with me these stories could never have been written.

To Marian Turski, editor of *Byli wówczas dziećmi*, a collection of childhood memories of World War II in Polish, who gave me permission to adopt Pavel's story.

To all those who have gone out of their way to help me by finding people to interview, by giving me at all times the opportunity to discuss children's inner life, and by accompanying my writing with editorial advice. From the many I only mention a few:

Joke Landsman, Pamela and Jim Knight, Rebecca Rass, Nechama Tec, Edith Velmans, Hester Velmans, Myriam Wenger, my sister, Anki, my husband, Peter, and my children, Andrea and Paulo.

"*Knowledge and reason only play a limited part in a child's life. Its interest quickly turns away from the real things in the outer world, especially when they are unpleasant, and reverts back to its own childish interests, to its toys, its games and to its fantasies. The danger in the outer world which it recognizes at one moment and to which it answers with its fear, is put aside at another moment.*"

—Anna Freud, *War and Children* (1943)

"*What does not kill us, makes us stronger.*"

—Nietzsche

About *A Child's War*

It may sound strange, but when I think of my own childhood years during the war I always get a good feeling inside. Today, half a century later, I still remember how terrible the war was, and I realize that it is only by a miracle that we survived. But even then, the first thing that comes back to me when I think of those times is the comforting love of my mother.

When World War II started I was five, and when it ended I was ten. My family was Jewish and we lived in Amsterdam. As soon as the first rumors arrived that our lives were threatened, my mother's attitude toward her children changed. Instead of spending her days playing bridge and organizing mundane outings with her friends, she made my sister and myself the center of her life. And the egocentric little girl I was secretly enjoyed suddenly receiving so much more attention.

Gradually, outings like going to the movies, parks, and swimming pools became forbidden to Jews. But I didn't mind a bit: staying at home seemed just as much fun. The growing food shortage didn't bother me either; I loved to be in the kitchen while my mother prepared the most delicious dishes out of the scarce ingredients.

In the evenings my parents would sit together, trying to figure out how to avoid being deported. With the door ajar I could follow their discussions from my bed. Once, when I heard my father say that he was considering sending only us children into hiding because he did not have enough savings to pay for all of us, I panicked. Being left behind and having to live with other people seemed to me the worst thing of all. I was much more afraid of that than of being sent to a camp with my parents. By that time I had heard many stories about concentration camps, that you could freeze from the cold and starve of hunger and that most people even died. But all that did not seem so terrible as long as we could stay together as a family.

At night, before falling asleep, I would try to imagine what our life would be like there. And the more often I thought about it the less frightening it seemed. I even became a little curious to see those barracks with long rows of bunks on top of each other. Sometimes I pictured myself playing outside with the other children, a thing which I hadn't been able to do for a long time. And then I also saw myself returning and telling everybody about life in the camp. The idea that I might not live to record it did not occur to me, because even though I knew that people were dying all over I was convinced that such a thing would never happen to me or to a member of my family.

By the second year of the war we were one of the few Jewish families in Amsterdam that had not yet been deported. We still lived in our apartment, but life became increasingly difficult. The police came to our house eighteen times to round us up. Every time my mother managed to convince them that we, the children, had a mysterious and contagious illness. She would bring out a fake doctor's certificate and go through lengthy explanations. When the police finally retreated, she would give them a piece of jewelry, an expensive coat, or an album of my father's stamp collection as a token of gratitude. In the meantime my sister and I had to keep quiet under the covers in our room, which had been generously sprinkled with disinfectant. After the first few times it became a terrible ordeal to jump into our beds as soon as somebody rang the bell. But we kept doing it, of course, and were pleased to be able to do something to help save the family.

Once the usual excuses did not work and we were taken to the Gestapo. My mother, in her determination to fight the impossible, asked to see the commandant and made up some incredible stories. The commandant couldn't have believed any of them, but he was incapable of resisting her charm. And at three o'clock in the morning, we found ourselves in the street. The only who was not pleased was me, because once outside I realized that I had left my doll's cradle behind!

In the fall of 1943 the Hungarian government allowed those Jews abroad who possessed a Hungarian passport to return to their country of origin. And so we found ourselves on a transport of about two hundred people traveling to Budapest. Our family and friends there had difficulty believing what we had gone through, and one aunt kept complaining that life in Budapest wasn't what it had been before, because there were no silk stockings to be found. She had no way of knowing that three months later she would find herself in Auschwitz.

Soon, the Germans broke their alliance with the Hungarians and took over completely.

My father was deported right away and my mother, my sister, and I were locked up in so-called Jewish houses guarded by Hungarian Nazis. The cruelty of the Hungarian Nazis deeply shocked me. It seemed outrageous that human beings could despise their own countrymen so deeply. Back in Holland it had been relatively easy to accept that the Germans were treating us badly. After all, they were the enemy. Here in Budapest, where the Hungarians behaved worse than the

Germans, I felt trapped because I believed that there was nobody we could trust and no place where we could hide.

Things happened fast in Hungary and before long we were caught up in the battle of Budapest. The bombardments were heavy and uninterrupted, but I quickly got used to them and was not afraid. On the contrary, in a strange way I found them exciting, especially at night because then the bombs looked like fireworks. Once, when we were staying in a fifth-floor apartment, we were woken by a deafening noise. The house was cracking and swaying, and the next morning we found out that the second floor had been completely destroyed. To know that I had survived, when the house had collapsed, gave me a sense of victory and reaffirmed my feeling of invulnerability.

To me the houses that had been destroyed by the bombings looked like enchanted castles full of hidden treasures. Once I found a crystal vase in the rubble that had remained perfectly intact. It was to me a proof that miracles did exist. I loved those ruins because they were not like any other playground. They were real houses that the grown-ups had built for themselves and then destroyed. And now that they had done that the ruins belonged to the children.

Being a girl did not stop me from collecting cartridges and shrapnel. They gave you such an exciting feeling when you held them in the palm of your hand. Those very objects had been used for real; they had made a difference in the big game of the war. Once I found a button of a uniform and I was sure that it had been lost by a soldier in the heat of battle. I couldn't stop thinking of him and kept wondering if he was still alive. How I admired those men in uniform. I felt that way whether I wanted to or not. Until my late teens I

[4]

remember finding men in uniform always virile and handsome.

My favorite game, playing father and mother, had lost its attraction. Since the war had begun, my parents hadn't even raised their voices to me. Playing father and mother without being able to scold your children was no fun at all. Why should I scold them when they behaved so well? They were just as well behaved as I was. When my parents asked me to do a chore I would obey immediately. Not because I liked it—I hated it just as much as before—but because I had to show them that I wasn't that spoiled little girl anymore. Shrewd as I was, I supposed they would do their utmost to let me stay with them if they knew that I wouldn't be a bother, even if I was only a child of seven. So instead of playing father and mother I became a devoted nurse for the wounded soldiers. It was a noble task because they were not ordinary patients, they were real heroes who had risked their lives for their wives and children. By taking care of them and saving their lives with the bullets flying around my ears, I became a heroine.

During the war the norms had changed. What had been "bad" before was "good" now and vice versa. I remember thinking how nice it was to be allowed to do things that were usually forbidden. Calling people nasty names was a sin, but when I said that the Germans were mean monsters, my parents didn't object. They only warned me not to repeat such things in front of other people. That just made it more exciting because it meant that I was big enough to share their secrets. And how elated we were, my sister and I, when we followed the example of other people who were looting the shops that had been broken into by the Russian soldiers. We knew very well that we were doing something forbidden, but that only added to our joy. Unfortunately our booty was disappointing—there wasn't anything left in the shops and we were very hungry. But all the same we were proud of the paper goods we had found, and we cherished them for a long time as a reminder of having been real looters.

I remember how my whole outlook changed when my father was deported. Convinced as I had been that nothing serious could happen to me or to anybody in my family, I suddenly sensed that my father might not be completely invulnerable after all. For the first time I was afraid, not of the Nazis nor of the bombings, but of the possibility that he might not return. I was only nine at that time, but I realized that without my father we would have lost the war whatever the outcome, because nothing could ever be as it was before.

During those dark days I became very dependent on my mother, and the fear of losing her as well constantly occupied my mind. One early morning the Nazis came to fetch her and a few other women to clean the nearby barracks. I was terribly anxious and was convinced that they used the cleaning up as an excuse to do something terrible to the women. When she hadn't returned in the evening I knew that I had been right. But late that night I was wakened by roars of laughter. My mother was there, telling the other roommates of her adventurous day. "And this German officer," I heard her say, "gave me a carpet beater and told me to beat an enormous rug. But I said that nobody had ever taught me how to do that and asked him to show me. And this idiot starts beating the rug like mad! And I stood there pulling faces behind his back and telling him how strong and how clever he was. . . ." When I heard her boasting like that, I became furious and indignant. My mother, the only adult person that I had left, was taking risks like that! Imagine what would have happened if another officer had seen her. They might very well have beaten her up and sent her to a

[6]

camp. I thought she had behaved scandalously for somebody who had to take care of two little children. She had behaved as if she were a child. If anybody had the right to behave like a child it was me! And even I would never do such a thing with the Germans. I was wiser than that, though I knew very well that it must have been fun and satisfying to do it. I was so angry that I resolved that this was going to be the first thing I would tell my father when . . . if . . . he came back. . . .

Actually I didn't even have to wait for my father's return, because I was constantly communicating with him in my mind. I kept reassuring him that I did my best to be brave and to be nice to mother even if she did foolish things. Naturally I trusted him, in his turn, to do the utmost to stay alive. And I also told him that I knew that this was very difficult for him because unfortunately it didn't depend on his own will alone. But even then, the least I could do was to promise him that he could count on my courage, because the worst thing would be if he came back and found that we hadn't made it to the end.

My secret conversations were my only way to be in touch with my father. In front of my mother and sister I didn't dare mention him. Who knew what they'd say—maybe they thought he'd never return, or even worse, maybe they knew something they didn't want to tell me. Instead of asking, I preferred to live with the benefit of the doubt.

As the siege went on, the Nazis realized that the Russians would win the battle sooner or later. Knowing that they in their turn would be the object of revenge, they put their last energies into murdering as many Jews as they could. During the night they emptied the houses near the Danube and took the people—men, women, elderly, and children—to the banks of the river. There they forced them to undress and walk for hours in the freezing cold. At dawn they executed them and threw the corpses into the Danube. This was the winter of 1944–45, one of the coldest of our century.

In her despair my mother decided that we would be safer hiding in an apartment than staying in the shelter with the others. And so we waited for the siege to end in one of the half-destroyed deserted apartments. Looking back I still wonder how we managed to survive without food and water. But nonetheless some of my best memories go back to the dreadful days we spent there.

The only useful thing that the inhabitants had left behind was an eiderdown. My mother put it around her shoulders, and my sister and I cuddled up to her. And while we sat there together I forgot the cold and the hunger and just felt the sweet tenderness of my mother. I was so happy when she whispered in my ear how she loved me and when she tenderly stroked my hair. Never before and never after have I felt so close to her.

None of us remembers how long it took before the Soviets came to liberate us. It must have been five or six weeks. During those endless days and nights I kept myself busy, communicating with my father, cuddling up to my mother, and inventing tricks to keep reality at a safe distance. When I heard my mother and sister complain about being hungry, when I heard them say we would die if it went on much longer, I told myself that they were exaggerating. We hadn't eaten anything for many days, that was true, but here we were, still alive, which proved that you could keep going without any food. And anyway, I reminded myself over and over, I still had my "iron reserve." I had managed to save a lump of salt, a few packets of sugar, and even a piece of bread, which I carefully preserved in my muff. Knowing that I had food in reserve was like a guarantee that I wouldn't die from hunger. At the same time it also kept me busy thinking of the moment that I would finally break into it and share it generously with my mother and sister.

I think that I was able to ignore my hunger by postponing it. And my trick worked perfectly, because even today I am not aware of having suffered real hunger. On a few occasions I did encroach on my "iron reserve." But I would only allow myself to do so if I knew that I could replace the eaten item by something else, preferably more nourishing. I must have connected emptying my muff with giving in, which meant the beginning of the end.

Another way of making myself feel better was to rub two stones, which I also kept in my muff, together. After some time they would start sparking and give a little light and warmth. And then there were the games of fantasy, when I would imagine myself a princess being taken by a handsome prince to his luxurious palace, where helpful servants were busy filling a tub with steaming hot water.

When I grew tired of cheating myself in my fantasy I would start bargaining with fate. I would spend hours and hours counting my buttons and then those of my mother and sister. The first one stood for yes, the second for no, and so on. If the last one said yes, the war was going to have a happy end. And somehow I always managed to count in such a way that the outcome reassured me.

My ritual games and secret prayers had worked: the miracle happened and my father returned. He had been in Bór, a labor camp in Yugoslavia. Only a few of his fellow prisoners survived; when the Germans knew they were going to lose, they started executing as many men as they could. It was sheer luck that the partisans came in time to liberate my father. When he finally arrived in Budapest, I had just turned ten. But even today I remember the moment I saw him again as the happiest of my life. I think that I must have sensed that fate had given our family a second chance.

We returned to Holland with one of the first Red Cross transports. And once we were back it seemed as if there had never been a war. There was no rubble in the streets, the electricity was working, and water came out of the taps. The schools had already started and the fact that I was Jewish did not seem to make any difference. I not only had the same rights but also the same obligations as the other children.

But my joy over all these novelties was shortlived because peace wasn't what I had imagined at all. I had imagined life after the war as a dream, that I would be free and able to do whatever I wanted. But now that peace was here at last, my parents suddenly started treating me like a little child. They came up with these stupid rules, like always answering with at least two words and letting older people help themselves first.

During the war, we children had always come first whenever my mother managed to lay her hands on some food. Now that there were delicacies to be had, they were passed around with quiet elegance. The guests were supposed to serve themselves first, and being the youngest, I had to wait until the end—till the very cookie I fancied was already taken! Though I was able to understand that this was the way things were supposed to be, I disliked formality profoundly and felt that after all my sufferings I didn't deserve to be treated like an ordinary child.

Life had become terribly boring. The routine of getting up every morning at the same time, going to school, returning home—day in day out, week in, week out—seemed totally senseless. The things we were taught had no practical value; they wouldn't be of any help if you had to protect yourself from danger. Instead of trying to catch up in class, I sat and daydreamed about those times when we were hiding and running and trying to save our lives. And although I knew that it wasn't right, I couldn't help hoping that something dramatic would happen again. A bomb, a fire, even a disaster like a flood would do. It wasn't that I wanted anybody to get hurt or killed, but I wanted to be part of something that happened, something that mattered, something that was exciting. Just once would do, just so I could feel once more what it had been like.

It took me several years to discover that activities like learning, sports, and arts could also present a challenge. But gradually I adapted and found that I wasn't so different from the other children. The only difference maybe was that I felt more compassion for those who suffered. One of my classmates, who was always singled out because her father had been a collaborator, became my best friend. When my parents found out they were furious, and however much I pleaded that it was unjust to blame children for the mistakes of their parents, they would not hear of it. Though I did sympathize with their point of view, I wouldn't give in: at the age of twelve I had decided that I would have to live according to my own moral standards.

This, in broad outline, is how I experienced the war. When my book* appeared in Holland I got many reactions from people who had also been children during World War II. A Dutch friend of mine confessed that she remembers that last winter, when people were dropping dead on the street from starvation, as the happiest time of her childhood. Being the younger of two she had always felt that her parents preferred her elder sister, who was an excellent student and always well behaved.

*Een Klein Leven, Bzztôh, The Hague, 1984.

[11]

During that winter the schools stayed closed, and while her sister did her homework my friend spent her time wandering outside. At the end of the day when she returned she was never empty-handed. There was always a piece of wood for the stove, a pocketful of rotten apples, or some frozen potatoes that she had found or stolen somewhere. And instead of scolding her for dirtying her coat her parents would rejoice and praise her for her talents.

My friend's example made me wonder about the criteria we parents use. About the reasons why we love our children and how these differ in war and peacetime. But above all it proved to me that children have their own way of perceiving things. My friend was not Jewish and she had lived through the war under totally different circumstances. But still her nostalgia for that terrible winter of starvation reminded me of my own feelings during the worst times of all.

In my book I also wrote about my fascination with the bombings and the soldiers' uniforms. It wasn't easy to do so, but my need to be honest was stronger than my fear of being criticized for it. My honesty paid off; a great number of people who had also been children during the war went out of their way to tell me that they had felt exactly the same way. Once I knew that my fascination with the bombings was not unusual I wondered if we who were children during the war had something in common. And if this was so, was it also something universal? In other words: would children from different national, religious, social, and political backgrounds basically *all* have felt the same way?

The only way to find out was to ask them directly, which meant interviewing a wide cross section of people who had been between five and ten years old during World War II. It also implied that I would have to work with distorted and romanticized memories. As my interest did not focus on historical facts, but principally on children's feelings, that didn't bother me. My own experience had taught me that the passing of time makes it easier to recognize one's truest feelings. It was only after forty years that some of my own feelings had lost their shamefulness and become endearing instead. Another advantage of interviewing adults would be that they could speak with hindsight about how the war had influenced them and what impact it had had on their lives.

For two and a half years—during most of which time I lived in Geneva—I searched for people who had been children in Europe during World War II. Altogether I interviewed over one hundred people from twenty-three different countries. It didn't make any difference to me if they were children of Jews, Resistance fighters, or Nazis. The only qualifications were their experience of the war and their age. The younger they had been, I found, the more their memories were loaded with emotion. Once they started recounting events that had occurred after their eleventh or twelfth year, they tended to rationalize more, and political considerations began making an appearance.

What amazed me most was their readiness to tell me, a total stranger, their most intimate childhood memories. The only thing I had told them about myself was that I too had been a child during the war and that my perception of the events was far different from what people expected it to be.

Most of the people I interviewed, and in particular those on whose true experiences the stories in this book are based, needed very little prompting. Their memories practically poured out of them without interruption. Once they had recounted their stories they seemed relieved, and later, when they had read the transcripts, they often expressed their gratitude; several of them said that for the first time they felt able to put it behind them. Most of them had never before told the whole story of their life during the war to anyone. Not because they had felt inhibited, but because nobody had shown genuine interest. And they had not wanted to burden their partners or children with those painful events.

Those interviewed were middle-aged, mostly professionals, and hard-working people. They gave me the impression of being well-balanced and strongly family-oriented.

In analyzing these one hundred stories I found that all the children, even under the most different circumstances, had largely had the same reactions and that they showed a consistent pattern. While physical deprivations like cold and hunger left them relatively indifferent, their main fear had been of being separated from their parents. The majority had not been afraid of the bombings; most children had even been fascinated by them. A few people remembered being afraid during air raids, but they said that the adults had passed their own fear on to them. Even in these cases the memories of the bombings were positive because during those fearful moments they had received enhanced affection. Those children who had been separated from their parents suffererd infinitely more than the others. But even then, most of them had managed admirably well to cope with their problems as long as there was still something to fight and hope for.

One of the few questions I asked the ex-children was how they felt today about the fact that they had to go through the war at such an early age.

I have always felt that the war had made me a stronger person. To know that I faced horrible dangers and still survived has given me self-confidence and the certainty that I can overcome whatever happens in everyday life. The war also gave me a true sense of appreciation. I see it as a privilege to be alive and can be happy with the most insignificant little things.

Of the hundred people, only three felt outright bitterness about having had to go through the war. All the others said that even though it was terrible, something positive had come out of it. Having to witness so many horrors and to confront so many problems made them aware of their inner strength. They also felt that the war gave them different values. Instead of taking everything for granted, like those who do not know what suffering is all about, they learned to be grateful for everything. This seemed to be a general attitude, independent of whether they had suffered a lot or a little. Actually those who had had the most difficult time seemed the most philosophical, as if they had been able to convert all the misery and sadness into an intense appreciation of the things that were good and beautiful.

Only a small minority expressed hate toward the Germans. When asked about the enemy, most people said that they had learned that nobody is entirely good and nobody is entirely bad, that there is some good and some bad in everybody, including themselves. And usually we concluded by saying that it would be wrong to point a finger at the enemy, without recognizing the potential danger in all of us.

—New York, 1989

FIORELLA

ITALY

"Mamma, why do I never get a banana anymore?"

"Because there is a war on, my little Fiorella."

The war had been going on for more than two months now. They kept on talking about the Fascists and the Communists, about Hitler and about Mussolini.

But not a word about bananas. That's why I asked:

"What do bananas have to do with the war?" Mamma smiled, and said, "That's much too complicated. You're too young to understand," and she gave me a kiss. With her it was always like that. She could never give me a decent answer. She'd give me a kiss instead. She hoped that then I'd leave her in peace. But it made me very angry. And also that she laughed at me. She thought that I was too little to understand what war was all about. But it wasn't true. I wasn't a baby anymore, I was almost seven.

Thank goodness Papa was so different. With him I could talk about anything I wanted to. And I didn't have to worry about making a fool of myself. He always took me seriously and treated me like an adult. Papa never read fairy tales to me, just stories from the *Divina*

[17]

Commedia by Dante. When I asked him what war really was, he said, "War is when people fight each other."

But they didn't fight just for fun. They had to have a reason. So I asked, "What do they do it for?"

"For freedom. Some people have certain ideas about freedom. And others have different ideas about freedom."

But I still didn't understand. "What is freedom?"

"Freedom is what every human being needs to lead a happy life. But the freedom of one person should not hurt the freedom of the other."

He explained things so beautifully. I hadn't understood it all, but I did know what he meant: as long as you didn't hurt anybody, you could do whatever you wanted. That was the freedom for which Papa and his friends were fighting. I said: "Papa, I want to help you. I want to fight with you."

From then on he always let me stay in the room when his friends came. Then he would take me on his lap and say: "Don't tell anybody what has been said here. Nor who you've seen here. But I want you to listen and to remember what you've heard."

Mamma was never at those meetings. Afterward, when they had left, she'd ask me who had been there and what they did. But I said, "I've promised Papa not to tell anyone." Then she'd get angry and shout at him: "You're teaching your daughter to lie!"

Papa wouldn't answer. He knew that she didn't like him being in the Resistance. The war was bad enough without that kind of game, as she called it. She thought he was taking too many risks. Papa understood that she was against it. Papa always understood everything.

We had to leave Milan when Papa's boss found out that he was in the Resistance. In Genoa he found a job right away, but a month later somebody told on him and he had to go underground. Papa's best friend was the director of the hospital, and he said; "I'll give you a room and we'll pretend you're sick. You come and go whenever you want."

Mamma and I lived on the fifth floor, and when there was an air raid we had to run down all those stairs as quickly as we could. The street would be full of people running here and there. They ran as fast as they could to the underground shelter. But when they got there, they'd stop short and hang around the entrance. They all waited until the very last moment to go down because the shelter was too small and terribly stuffy.

Once, as we got to our places, there was a terrible noise outside. A bomb must have exploded nearby. The people threw themselves at the entrance, but it was too small for all of them at once. They fought like crazy to get inside. They yelled and hit and kicked as hard as they could. I was thrown to the ground, and all I could see were arms and legs and faces with bulging eyes and wide-open mouths. They stepped on me, and I felt somebody's heel cut into my shoulder. It hurt terribly, but I didn't want to scream. I didn't want to be like these people. What kind of people were they? They came to save their lives and ended up trampling each other to death!

An old lady who had been crushed underfoot died. When Mamma heard that she decided that from now on we would spend the nights in a tunnel near our house. At least that way we wouldn't have to rush down all those stairs. Some nights we ran to the shelter eighteen times!

I loved being in the tunnel. There were whole families living there. They'd sit around eating and drinking, and afterward they'd start singing. And all the children played together. Whenever they asked me to join in I always said yes. It was fun being with kids who were so different. I knew that Mamma didn't really like my playing with them, just because they were so different. But she didn't say anything because she knew there was nothing she could do about it.

At night, when I was lying on my màt, I watched the trams ride through the tunnel. I watched the people too. There were people walking up and down all night long. If you listened long enough you could hear how they all lifted and put down their legs at the same time. And then, when you closed your eyes, you felt the ground move up and down, like waves. I loved it, to be rocked asleep like that.

But we had to leave Genoa. We couldn't buy a thing with our ration books and didn'thave enough money for the black market. In the country there would be more food, and there wouldn't be any bombs. But so what? I wasn't scared, and I didn't mind being hungry. In the country I'd see Papa even less. At least in Genoa I could go and visit him in the hospital. Being with Papa always made me feel better. Then I'd know all this misery had a reason. Because after the war, when the Fascists had lost, everything would be different.

Sometimes Papa told me about the things he did in the Resistance. One day, he had to deliver a gun someplace and they came up with a clever trick. His friend put Papa's leg in a plaster cast with the gun inside! Who would question somebody's broken leg? Poor Papa, for three and a half hours he walked like that! I loved those stories, they made me feel proud. And also relieved, because of the happy ending.

We found a big room in the village street above the pastry shop. Or what had once been the pastry shop. All that was in the shop window now were empty bonbon boxes and dusty porcelain statuettes. Behind that hung a curtain, and that's where the baker's family lived. There were two little girls and a boy my age.

[20]

The boy, Giorgio, helped us carry the suitcases upstairs. When he put them down, he stayed where he was and took out a red handkerchief. He started to blow his nose as if he had a terrible cold, but I knew that he was just pretending. When he finished he wiped his face all over and said, "Your father didn't come?"

"He had to stay in Genoa. In the hospital."

"Is he very sick?"

"Yes, kind of . . ."

"How long's he been sick?"

"A year and a half. But sometimes they let him go out."

"My father isn't around much either."

"Where is he?"

"In the mountains."

"With the partisans?"

How stupid to blurt it out! But when I saw him playing with the red handkerchief it made me think of the partisans. And then, when he said that his father was in the mountains, I was nearly sure that he was on our side. Giorgio bent over and whispered, "Want to help us?"

"Oh yes, please!"

And then he said loudly, so that Mamma could also hear it, "If you feel like it, I could come and pick you up tomorrow afternoon. Then you can meet the rest of us."

Giorgio and his friends were helping the partisans. Just before you got to the village there was a big hill, and from there you had a good view over the road. It was the lookout. The children stayed on the hill all day, and if they saw something suspicious they were supposed to run down screaming and yelling as hard as they could. Then the men in the village could quickly hide.

Once, when playing on the hill, we saw military

trucks below us on the road. We hadn't seen them coming! Quickly we ran down the hill, shouting loudly. My foot got caught and I fell down, head over heels. There was a silence. . . . What had happened to the others? Then there was a crack and next to me I heard a thump. . . . I felt spatters on my face. I wiped myself and saw my hands. They were full of blood and strange white flecks. Giorgio! He was lying on the ground, right next to me, his head all in pieces . . . with stuff coming out. . . . I couldn't stand the sight of it. Home! Home! Mamma, Mamma, Mamma, Mamma!

Mamma immediately undressed me and put me in the tub. Only a minute later they were banging on the door. She shouted, "Who is there?"

"Open up! Open up! Open!"

"Coming, coming. . . . Just a second."

She got me out of the tub and carried me over to the bed. Two men in uniform entered the room.

"We are looking for partisans. We know they are here."

"There's only my daughter here, and she is sick in bed."

They looked in all the corners, in the closet, and under the bed. I was afraid that they would find my dirty clothes. But Mamma had managed to bundle them up, out of sight.

In the evening Giorgio's mother came. She wanted to know everything; what we had been doing that day and what he had said. I realized that those things had suddenly become important. Giorgio had been the same as ever, but for her it made a difference because it had been the last time. So I tried to tell her everything as well as I could. I kept asking myself if she wanted to know the other thing as well: how in the end he had been lying there covered all over with gore. But luckily she didn't want to hear about that.

[22]

A few weeks later Papa came to visit. He had heard about the accident and was proud of me for having helped the partisans. It hadn't surprised him of his own Fiorella. When he said that, my stomach turned over from fear that he might ask me all kinds of questions. I couldn't talk about Giorgio, even with Papa. I dreamt about it every night, and in the daytime I kept seeing Giorgio, the way he'd been lying there. However hard I rubbed my eyes, that smashed head with blood and white gobs wouldn't go away. But Papa had come about something different.

He said, "I want to take you somewhere, Fiorella."

We walked a long way until we came to a forest. He said we were safe there, then looked for an open space between the trees and put a gun in my hand. It was terribly heavy, and I nearly dropped it. But Papa said, "I want you to learn how to use it." He showed me how to load it and how to pull the trigger. It was very difficult, and I was very clumsy, but he said there was no hurry—that I should just keep practicing until I could do it. When I got a little better, he said, "Now we'll bury it. You have to remember this place and when you need it you can come and get it."

We got a message: we should go to Dr. Arrigoni's right away. Papa told us that Dr. Arrigoni was also against the Fascists and that we could trust him. When we rang the bell he took us immediately into his office and told Mamma, "Your husband has been arrested. Somebody in the hospital betrayed him. He was probably taken to the municipal prison." Mamma stood there, not saying a thing. She just looked straight ahead of her, staring outside. As if there was something to see out there in the fields. Dr. Arrigoni took a roll of lire out of his pocket and stuffed it into her handbag. How old her bag looked, all flabby and the color worn off. The clasp that used to shine so brightly was dull and gray. Strange that it only struck me now. Did this mean we were poor? It was the first time I wondered about that.

Mamma lowered her head and began to cry softly. She said, "Thank you, doctor. Thank you. You are a good man. . . ." and left the room without looking up. When she was at the door Dr. Arrigoni laid his hand on her shoulder and said, "You have to let me know if there is something you need. Don't forget that you can always count on me."

On our way home I thought: Dr. Arrigoni sent for us because he had a message. He had to inform us of something we didn't know yet. But that wasn't so! I knew it before he had said it. I had known it all the time. Back when we were still in Milan. But I'd never wanted to think about it. I just didn't want to know it. That's why it had still happened so unexpectedly.

At the entrance to the prison there was a woman sitting behind a little window. She was screwing the top off a thermos. When she saw us she just went ahead and began filling her cup. I was sorry we had arrived at this very moment, but it was too late now to go away. The woman cocked her head to find out what we wanted.

Mamma said, "Good morning. Uh, excuse me. Please . . . I just wanted to know if my husband is here. His name is Guipponi, Ernesto Guipponi."

How politely she spoke. She did her very best. It hurt me to hear her talk like that. She never did that. The woman behind the window put a piece of bread in her mouth and said, "That traitor? I don't even know if he's still alive!"

Mamma took a step backward in fright. She had wanted to ask so many questions, but now she knew that it made no sense. There was so much hatred in that voice that there was nothing left to hope for.

[24]

I had never heard anybody speak in a tone like that. I didn't know that people could hate that way. Mamma had always said that the world was full of bad people, but I had never wanted to believe her. I couldn't imagine that somebody could be totally bad, through and through. But she'd been right. Now I had to admit it. But that wasn't all. There was something else, something that was even worse. The woman was Italian. She was not German, so she wasn't even our real enemy. The first person I really hated was an Italian. And that was the worst, because you shouldn't hate somebody from your own country. But she was a Fascist, which meant that she was with Hitler and Mussolini, against us. That's why I had to hate her. But it would have been a lot easier if she had been German.

There was a wooden bench nearby, and we walked over to it. We didn't want to leave yet; we wanted to wait. What we were waiting for we didn't know. But who could tell?—someone else might take that woman's place. Somebody who would give us some information. Maybe she was very tired; she might have been sitting there all night.

I heard something. Was it my imagination? Were those screams? No, they couldn't be! But they kept coming back. Mamma just sat there, all hunched up. I didn't dare to ask, but I still wanted to know: "Do you think that they . . . Papa?"

"Yes . . ." she sobbed and started to cry. I put my arm around her shoulder, and we sat like that. But I didn't believe that it was Papa. Nor anybody else either, because although there were other prisoners in there too, these were not human voices. Nobody could scream that loudly. They must have used instruments that imitate sounds, just to frighten us.

Suddenly it was quiet. It was nearly five o'clock. If we wanted to catch the last train we had to leave. But

[25]

then it started again, even louder than before. Though it was hardly possible. Or had we already forgotten? We couldn't leave now. We *had* to stay.

A bell rang. It sounded like a siren. A man with a big bunch of keys walked toward us. He opened the door and said, "It's eight o'clock. You can't stay here any longer."

Everybody was excited and was talking about the liberation. The war couldn't last much longer. The Fascists had lost, and we had won. That was nice, but I couldn't be happy. I didn't feel anything special.

One evening we heard a car stop. It was a taxi and somebody got out. Papa! Papa! He was back! It couldn't be! But it was! Suddenly the war was over for me and I could be as excited about the liberation as everyone else.

Papa wanted to lie down because he felt a little tired. I went to sit next to him and touched his hand. But he pulled it back as if he'd had an electric shock. I asked him if I had hurt him and he replied: "Yes, but it's not your fault." He lifted his head and said: "Fiorella, I hardly recognize you. You've gotten so tall. You're getting to be a real young lady. And *what* a young lady. I didn't know that I had such a beautiful daughter."

"Papa, Papa, you are back. I am so happy!"

He had fallen asleep and I could look at him now, silently. How he had changed! So old and skinny and *ugly*. When that word came into my mind I was ashamed of myself. It wasn't his fault, was it? And after all, what did it matter? Even if he were the *ugliest* man in the world, he would still be my father and I would love him just as much! I saw the hand that I had tried to touch before. His fingers were twisted and swollen and there were black spots where his nails should have been.

[26]

He made a strange noise during his sleep. It was like a kind of coughing and a little fluid was coming out of his mouth. First just a little bit, but then more and more, and suddenly there was a squirt of blood. I heard Mamma cry beside me and I pulled a little closer. But I couldn't comfort her.

Dr. Arrigoni said that it would be wiser to take him to the hospital. They might still be able to do something for him there. But after one week he had a terrible bleeding and the next day another one. Papa died on April 26, the day of the liberation. My papa had been the best and the sweetest one of all. In ten years, he had taught me everything I knew.

Today Fiorella says:

"The moment I saw that little boy with his brains all over the place stays engraved in my mind. It is like an open wound, and whenever I have a problem I refer to it. In my dreams I relive the scene and see myself running home covered with blood. But telling my story has worked like a catharsis. Afterwards I had nightmares again, but somehow I was always able to get out of them, and the people I had seen dead were alive again. I saw them alive and they were happy. Then they returned to oblivion, but good oblivion, without black thoughts.

"By having me sit in on his secret meetings, my father awoke in me a sense of responsibility. It worked as a seed that grew inside me. Maybe it was a sad childhood for that reason. Because being so young I was already quite old. But when I think of the child I was back then, I have no regrets. I don't mind having lost the innocence of childhood."

Fiorella is a translator and lives in Milan, Italy.

ROBIN

ENGLAND

Ripping good news on the BBC! England has declared war on the Jerries. Finally! They should have done that as soon as Hitler swallowed up Czechoslovakia. But no, those chaps in Whitehall couldn't make up their minds. Mr. Chamberlain had to wait until Hitler had invaded Poland. Perhaps it's just as well that Hitler did that. At least it made Mr. Chamberlain decide at last.

We know all there is to know about the Jerries. Dad was in the trenches right through World War I. Those three medals he has weren't for nothing. Nobody knows as well as Dad what dirty scum those Jerries are.

There's a photograph of Dad in his Coldstream Guards uniform on our mantelpiece. I often look at it and wonder if I'll look as smashing in my uniform as he does in his. Will I be just as handsome as he is? In the photo he's twenty-one, and I'm only seven now, so it's hard to tell.

I hope there will be another war when I grow up. Because I don't see the point of being in the army without being in a real fight. And as a pilot they wouldn't let me drop any bombs if it was peacetime. I want to join the RAF. I'm not the only one, of course, and I hope they'll have enough bombers to go around. All the boys in my form want to become pilots. Except Jeremy, of course. He's going to be a teacher. But he doesn't count. He isn't a boy, he's just a sissy.

When I ask Dad how many Jerries he shot he won't say. Of course it doesn't really matter—it isn't important at all. Peter is so proud that his father killed sixteen. He never stops boasting about it. If only I could say: "*My* Dad killed seventeen" (or, even better: nineteen), he'd have to keep his big mouth shut.

Our bomb shelter is at the top of Mum's rock garden. We'll never hear the end of it! She keeps saying that it took her twelve years to get it looking nice. Women have no idea what war is all about and the sorts of sacrifices you have to make. The girls I know are like that too. I hope they're not *all* like that, or I'm never going to get married.

The shelter is like a room, only with very thick walls and no windows. After the war we could use it as a workshop. Or even as a garage, if we have a car. You can climb on top and from there you can see the sea and the walls of the shipyard where my Uncle Jack works. He told me that Barrow-In-Furness is where they make the very best submarines.

Thank goodness we don't have Mr. Johnson as often as before. What a rotter! It's incredible how that chap can get all worked up about little things while his country is at war! Ridiculous. And he's always out to get me. The other day he said: "Robin! How much is seven times eight?"

Now I know my tables, all of them. Back to front and inside out. Seven is the only one I have a little trouble with. Eight's no problem. But you see, I wasn't sure if eight times seven was exactly the same as seven times eight. And then I wasn't completely sure if it was sixty-five or fifty-six. So I said, "I think I know, sir. But I'm not quite sure. . . ."

"Robin, this isn't the first time that I'm testing you on the seven times table."

"Yes, sir. And I do know it, it's just that it's rather difficult. Once you get to the middle—"

"Which of you chaps can tell me what seven times eight is?"

"The same as eight times seven," I heard the sissy say.

"And how much is that, Jeremy?"

"Fifty-six, sir."

Fifty-six! I knew it! Why hadn't I said it? Why did I always have to mix it up with sixty-five? Well . . . who cares. . . . Mr. Johnson can get stuffed.

These days we have more important things to learn than the seven times table. Like first aid. With that you'd better not make any mistakes. If you give somebody too loose a bandage he could bleed to death. And if you make it too tight he could lose his arm, because you'd cut off the blood. Miss Lockwood explained it all to us. If I know the reason I have to do something, I don't have any trouble remembering. We practiced with real bandages, and one time Miss Lockwood let me bandage her arm. She told me I'd done rather a good job. She should know. She's a real nurse with a uniform and all. I'm glad there are women like that, too.

After school they're teaching us how to put out fire bombs. We each get our own pump and our own bucket. There's a huge mountain of sandbags in the playground. When the gym teacher leaves we always stay to play war. The team that captures the sandbags wins. The only one who never joins in is Jeremy. He hates his gas mask, too. It is rather a nuisance having it dangling around your neck all the time. But who'd make a fuss about that! Anyway, Mum always puts a pack of sweets

[31]

inside, in case of emergency. She gets mad when I've eaten it. But I know that she'll just put another pack in again. Because she'd never risk not putting one in, of course.

Sometimes, in my bed, I can hear the buzzing of the German bombers. It's very soft and it comes in waves. It sounds as if they're growling: "We are very close, but from down there you can't see us." Those dirty cowards only dare come here after dark. But then at last, all at once you hear *pom, pom, pom, pom, pom, pom . . .*—very fast—and then you know that our antiaircraft guns are going off. And then you hear the sirens howling and you have to run to the bomb shelter.

I wish Joyce would start to cry, because then I could say: "Don't be a baby! Why would they want to bomb *our* house? It's only the shipyard they're after." But Joyce isn't crying. She is quite brave, actually. That's not so hard when you're sitting on your mother's lap.

Dad usually goes to the kitchen to make some tea. But tonight he's staying in here with us. The bombing has never been this bad. Even if there's no tea tonight, will there be a biscuit anyway? The biscuits are stored in here. That's why I like the air raids. But I won't ask. I'll wait. Joyce will start whining for one soon enough.

But Joyce doesn't seem to be too interested in biscuits tonight. She's just listening to the noise of the bombs and watching the flame of the paraffin lamp, which is flickering and keeps wanting to go out because of the shaking.

At last something happens! Dad lights two matches. He holds them above the tobacco in his pipe and his whole face starts to move. Then he inhales deeply, chews quietly on his pipe, and says: "Looks like we'll be here for a while. So why don't I go make us a pot of tea anyway." And before Mum can open her mouth he's gone. He makes a dash for it—with the bombs falling all around! What a hero, my Dad is. He isn't afraid of anything. I won't be, either, when I'm big.

On the last day of school we got our cards. They're splendid, with your photo on the left with a stamp across part of it, and to the right is written things like your name, your age, place of birth, religion, and the color of your hair. We had to sign underneath, and then Mr. Johnson gave us each a transparent case with a cord through it. He told us it was to carry the cards around our neck. That's typical of Mr. Johnson, inventing such a thing. We aren't babies, are we? *He* doesn't wear *his* papers around his neck, does he?

All the parents came to the station to say good-bye. Some mothers were crying, but my Mum didn't, luckily. I was glad when the train finally started moving. More and more children started yammering. I couldn't stand it. Especially not now, with everything so exciting. I'd never been on such a long journey, and I was awfully curious to find out where I would end up. A castle, I hoped, with a drawbridge and a moat around it. I'd often had dreams about it. And why not? This could be my lucky day. They had plenty of castles where we were going.

If only I didn't have such a bellyache. I don't even know if it's real pain, it just feels like a big, heavy rock in there. And then suddenly a stitch in my side. Oh—I can't stand it! Everything starts to spin and I don't even know where I am. And then once I open my eyes again I feel even worse. Because I see that I'm still lying here in this cold attic.

Last night I stared into the flame of the candle for a very long time. I kept thinking about Mum and Dad. I even prayed. I don't usually. Not because I don't want to (Mum told me to say my prayers every night), but I just forget. I asked Our Father to send the Luftwaffe over here to bomb this house. But Our Father didn't hear me because nothing happened. Nothing ever happens here. It's so far away and dull that nobody is interested. Not even Our Father.

I have to call her Auntie Jane but I don't feel like it. When she brings me my food she asks me how I'm feeling. But I'm not feeling any better and I still can't eat a thing. When I ate three spoonfuls of soup it just came right out again. And not only that little bit of soup, but a lot more. I don't understand how that can happen, if you haven't eaten for days. I really must be very sick. If it goes on much longer they'll have to send me home. Because they don't even have a doctor here. They've never even heard of doctors here.

Of course it had to be Jeremy who got the castle. He gets driven to school in a Rolls Royce every day, like a little lord. Lucky fellow! And we have to *walk* three and a half miles each way! But the worst is, *he* isn't even enjoying it. The only thing he can tell us is that the rooms are big and cold and that the Duke and the Duchess are never there. When I asked him how many gun slits there were, he said he hadn't counted and he couldn't care less. He just wants to go home. Well, what can you expect from such a Mummy's boy?

After school we have to help sweep out the stable and take care of the little lambs. They're a lot of work. They're the stupidest animals there are. But such sweet things! And I'm very good with them, they listen to me. The other day, a mother sheep died. And they let me feed the little one with a bottle. And now it's my job to feed him until he's big enough to do it by himself.

Auntie Jane is a wonderful cook. Every morning we have bacon and eggs. The eggs are still warm when you go and collect them from underneath the hens.

[34]

At night we listen to the radio. The war is going splendidly. We are bombing all the German cities: Bonn, Frankfurt, Hamburg, even Berlin! More than a million Jerries dead already. And a good thing too, those dirty Jerries. It's about time someone taught Hitler a lesson.

There are some strange goings-on here. Every morning at six o'clock a military truck stops in front of the house and five men get out. They stay here all day and are picked up again in the evening. They're prisoners of war. That means they're soldiers who lost and were taken prisoner. And they just let those fellows walk around here, if you please! No guards! Auntie Jane and Uncle Jack had better watch out! Those chaps do work quite hard, that's true. And they don't get paid either, but still . . . they're the enemy, aren't they? They would have killed us if they could have, wouldn't they? And we could have and we didn't! We took them prisoner and brought them all the way back to England. And now that they're here we act as if they aren't even our enemies, but just ordinary workmen.

Auntie Jane lets them eat with us. She says that makes it easier for her. The first day I was really rather nervous, even though I'm pretty brave. I made sure to sit at the other end of the table. What if one of them asked me something? Then I'd have to answer and look him in the eyes.

But I've gotten used to them by now and they're very quiet. When they do talk it's to each other, and I can't understand them anyway. There are three Germans and two Italians.

One time I was walking near the barn. They're allowed to rest there after supper. One of the Germans was cutting a piece of wood with a knife. He did it so fast and so neatly that I couldn't help watching. Of course he noticed and winked at me to come closer. It wouldn't be right to run on now. It was too late. When I came closer I saw that he'd carved a little dog. He stretched out his hand and said: "For you. Take it."

It was a frightfully good dog. How do you do that, make a dog out of just a piece of wood? But of course I couldn't take it, so I said, "No. No."

"You not like it?"

"Yes, I do. That's not it . . ."

How could I tell him what I was thinking? So I just turned and started to walk away. But he called after me, "I make different thing for you! Tell me what."

"I don't know."

I looked at him as I said it. It was the first time. It was different from what I'd thought. His eyes were very ordinary, they weren't frightening at all. In fact they didn't even look unfriendly. He asked: "A bird? A cat? An Indian?"

I love Indians. Winnetou's my favorite. Before I knew it, I'd said, "Yes!"

"Good," he said. "But you must help. I need big piece of wood."

In the woodpile I found the top of an old butter-churn. He started on it right away. How fast his hand moved! I loved looking at it.

"You learn also?" he asked, and he took my hand so fast that I didn't even have time to think about it. But it wasn't scary at all, his hand was big but felt very light. When he started carving again it seemed as if I were the one doing it. It was smashing to see the mouth come out, slowly. Then he said, without stopping, "You get paint. And horse's hair. Beautiful Indian!"

At school everyone is jealous of my mask. And they all want to know who gave it to me. It's none of their business! They'd really let me have it if they heard I got if from a prisoner of war. And a German one, too. And that he made it specially for me.

It's not that I'm ashamed of it. Not at all. But they wouldn't understand. They only see the Germans as wicked scum. They don't see that they're just people, too. Ordinary people, just like us.

Barrow-In-Furness looks totally different from before. Everything has been flattened and all you can see are ruins. Shrapnel and fragments of shells everywhere. I got a beautiful collection in a few days.

Down the street two houses have been destroyed. They look just like two old forts, and after school we go there with a whole gang and play. We hide behind the walls that are still standing and pelt each other with stones. All you have to do is pick them up. There are heaps, all over.

I also have some live cartridges that I bought from two chaps who broke into the RAF armory. One of them even picked a real Sten gun. At first I wouldn't believe him, but he showed it to me. He kept it locked inside his desk at school. Taking it home would be too risky.

One day when I got home I saw the *Daily Express* lying open on the table. Normally, we weren't allowed to touch it until Dad had read it. Had *Mum* all of a sudden gotten interested in politics?

Closer up I saw some names in big letters: Auschwitz, Mauthausen, Bergen-Belsen. Never heard of them. And, lower, lots of photographs. Strange photographs. Loads of dead people piled in a ditch. And living skulls looking at you with huge eyes. What was this? I didn't understand! And what about those spooky figures standing behind the barbed wire? And those bald people in striped clothes? There were also photographs of big steel doors. The captions said they were the ovens where

[37]

they'd been burning—people. Fancy! Burning people in ovens? What a load of nonsense! Who'd dream up something like that? It must be a joke. But a very bad joke. They only did it to sell newspapers. Now that the war is over, the papers are going to go out of business. My own Dad says so.

But I keep having to look at those photos, over and over again. They are so strange, so different. Maybe that's why I find them so interesting. Once Dad was done with the paper I asked him if I could cut them out. Now I have saved them and look at them every time I want to have this weird feeling again.

Today Robin says:

"The war remains perhaps the most memorable period of my life. I feel it has been a real foundation, a reference point. Without the war I would see my life as rather dull. But when I look back now, I come to this great plateau—crowded with marvelous events—which is this experience of the war. I wouldn't have missed it. Highly positive.

"My encounter with the prisoners of war was an interesting experience, too. To discover that people I feared and hated—that I had been taught to fear and hate—were just like us, and not at all the gruesome, terrifying enemies one heard talk about. I suppose this was one of my first lessons in understanding other people, in not accepting first impressions as complete and final and irrevocable."

Robin is a journalist. He has two children and lives with his wife in Geneva, Switzerland.

MARICA

RUMANIA

"How stupid of me," Mrs. Shapiro cries. "I nearly forgot to give the child some sweets." She turns around and hurries back into the room. Mr. Shapiro stays with us in the hall. But he and Tata* don't speak anymore. The maid brings us our coats and Tata takes them from her. Now here comes Mrs. Shapiro, she's almost running. She holds out a big box of chocolates for me and says, "Just help yourself, dear . . . I don't even know your name." "My name is Marica," I say, and I take a bonbon. Not the biggest one—on purpose—and a kind of which there are many. "Another one for the road," she says. And when she sees I'm not moving, she takes a few chocolates out of the box and stuffs them into my pocket.

"Perhaps you'd like one too?" She asks suddenly, looking at Tata. Tata answers: "No, thank you, Mrs. Shapiro." Mrs. Shapiro says, "Too bad, they are very good." Tata nods at her and at Mr. Shapiro and says, "Come darling, we have to go."

*"Father" in Rumanian.

[41]

Out on the street I ask Tata, "What should I do with those chocolates?"

"Just eat them."

"But they are bad people."

"That's the way the world is. Don't let it bother you."

"Tata?"

"Yes, my sweetheart."

"Are we going home now? Or do we still need to see other people?"

"We're going home, my angel. I've been everywhere."

Tata never told me why he was going to see all those people. But he didn't have to, I was there and could see for myself. He asked them if they could lend him some money because all of his money was in the business. And the Germans had taken away his business because he was a Jew.

But everywhere the answer was *no*. And not because those people didn't have enough money. They actually had a lot of money. When we were at Mr. Weinberger's, he went to the wall and started turning a knob until suddenly a tiny little door opened up. And when that little door was open, I saw a hole, and in it there were blocks of gold! I could hardly believe my eyes. Later, when I asked if what I'd seen was real, Tata said it was. Mr. Weinberger is very rich, but I still wouldn't want him to be my father. He is much too old and has a crooked nose with big holes and dirty hairs sticking out.

There is a suitcase on the bed and Tata and Mama are putting all kinds of things in it. When I ask what they are doing, Tata says, "Why don't you pack your toys in the meantime? You can take whatever you can carry by yourself."

I go to the room and take my toys out of the closet

and the drawers. Most of the time, when Tata and Mama tell me to do something, I ask, "Why?" but this time I don't ask. Because I know it won't help anyway. They are so busy right now that they don't have time to explain things.

But it's okay for me to be by myself for a while. I am four years old already, and not at all a baby anymore. You know what? I'll show them that I can pack my toys easily all by myself.

I do have a lot of toys. And I'll have to carry them all by myself. But I can't leave them behind, just like that, can I? So—how shall I do it?

I guess there are lots of things I never play with. Those will just have to stay here for now. I'll just take along the toys I love best.

Like my darling rocking horse. But he is much too big to carry! And my little stove? I just got all the new pans. . . . And my doll's pram?

I know! I have an idea! I'll stuff all my toys into the doll's pram. Then I won't have to carry them.

Tata calls, "Marica, are you done?" "Yes, Tata," I say proudly. "Everything is in the pram." "Come on! Hurry up!" he says. "We have to be in the ghetto before four o'clock."

In the ghetto they put us in a room with at least thirty other people—strangers, and we don't know any of them. Some are very old. And there are little children who keep crying all the time.

"Tata?"

"What is it, Marica?"

"When can we go home?"

"I don't think we'll go home very soon."

"But we can't stay here, can we?"

"Anything is possible, my darling. The Germans can do whatever they want with us. They could leave us here. But they could also come and get us."

[43]

"I hope that they will come and get us soon."

"Don't say that, sweetheart. If they come and get us, it will be to take us to a camp."

It is nearly dark and we still have the Dnjestr to cross. And I am so tired from all that standing. We have been standing here all day, waiting for the boat.

"Marica! Here comes the boat!" says Mama.

"I don't believe it."

"Yes, yes it is! Let me lift you up. Then you can have a look."

I see a boat alongside of the shore. Could that be it? It is so small. . . . The boat I had imagined was not like that at all: that one was like the white one I once saw in a magazine.

People are already climbing on board. But the boat is almost full already. There is much too little room for all of us. And the soldiers keep shouting all the time: *"Raum machen! Schnell! Schnell!"** More and more people are crowding on. We are just about the very last to climb on board. And we are standing at the very edge.

I am so afraid that we're going to drown. But I won't cry. I press my Nyú-Nyú against me. He is so wonderfully soft, and yet so sturdy, too. Lucky for me that I have him with me. "If I fall in the water, you'll save me—won't you?" I whisper in his ear. I repeat it over and over, very fast, over and over again, so that nobody can hear me.

The people are screaming. They cry: "We're sinking!" And then suddenly a stern voice shouts: "Don't panic! If we all stay calm, nothing's going to happen." Tata says, "Grab my belt and hold on tight."

Something plops into the water. I look up and Tata says, "Don't worry, my darling. It was only my coat."

*"Make room! Hurry! Hurry!"

Dr. Weiss has promised to come and have a look at Tata. He happens to be here in Mogilev* too. Tata has had typhoid for so long, and he just isn't getting any better.

Where is Dr. Weiss? Why isn't he here yet? I know he has to work very hard. But can't he come and take a look at Tata, just for a moment? If he waits too long he may not be able to help him anymore.

Tata is asleep all the time. At least that's what I think he's doing because he never says anything. Except last night. Last night he suddenly started talking very loudly. Mama said it was because of the fever. What he was saying was all mixed up—you couldn't understand a thing. The only word that kept coming back was *"Palestine."* In the ghetto he had met a man who said that you could go to Palestine if you had family there. And Tata has a sister there, Aunt Leila.

Here's Dr. Weiss! But . . . he looks so thin . . . and he hasn't shaved. . . . He used to be such a good-looking doctor. But what do I care? As long as he makes Tata better.

The doctor leans over Tata. With his thumbs he pulls Tata's eyelids up and then pushes them back again. Then he lifts Tata's arm, feels his wrist, and folds his arm over his chest.

He looks at Tata and thinks for a long time. Then he stretches his back and sighs a deep sigh. "I'm afraid that it's already happened," he says to Mama.

I'm not allowed to be there when they come and get Tata. That's why I am standing here, outside. But I am so big now that I can look inside, through the window. I see two men putting him down on a big plank. And

*Camp in the Ukraine.

[45]

then I can just see his hair as they carry him out. There's hardly any left because it all fell out from typhus.

Dear Tata . . . Now you're gone. . . . Will I ever see you again? Can that be true? You really won't come back again? I can't imagine it. Somewhere, I'm sure, we will meet again. I don't know where. But somewhere, there must be such a place. There must be.

Tata must have caught cold standing in line for water. Every morning in the cold, without his warm coat. If only he could have kept his coat he would never have gotten sick. And if I hadn't taken along my Nyú-Nyú there would have been enough space. And he wouldn't have had to let his coat fall into the water.

Grandma is in the same barracks as Aunt Judith, Aunt Nina, Uncle Otto, and Bruno. I think they have a lot more to eat than us. I don't know how they get it. Maybe from that friend of Aunt Judith's. She met somebody here who works in the kitchen. But when I go there I never get anything. Once, Aunt Nina gave me a potato, but she said, "Just this once. I can't give you something every time."

The other day, I saw Grandma chewing on something. But when I asked her what it was, she said, "Nothing. I'm only doing that because my teeth are bothering me." When I came home I said to Mama, "Why doesn't she just say that she doesn't want to give me anything?"

Mama has gotten a whole loaf of bread. Great! For once we have something too. But we have to watch out that they don't steal it. When there was nobody in the barracks Mama sewed half of it inside the mattress. And the rest we carry in our pockets.

The bread came from a German who lives near the camp. Mama gave her the dress that Tata had bought

[46]

her in Paris that time. The only thing she still has left to exchange is her silk nightgown trimmed with lace.

All that time we didn't have a thing. And now that we have the bread, suddenly we also have some money—sent to us by Uncle Dan in Bucharest. Uncle Dan and Aunt Anna are still living there in their beautiful villa. They're really lucky, because in Bucharest there is hardly any war.

Mama has given me some money. I walk to the fence to buy something. The peasants there have so many good things to eat: sauerkraut, pickles, and sometimes poppyseed cakes. . . . The cake is the most expensive, but that's what I really want.

Yum . . . It tastes so good. . . . It reminds me of before the war. . . .

Mama comes into the barracks. When she sees me sitting on my wooden bed she asks, "Is it good?" "Great," I say. "It tastes like before . . ." "Well-done," she says, and she asks me for the change.

I look for the change, but I can't find it anywhere. Where is it? It can't have disappeared just like that! I look everywhere, but it's gone.

Mama starts to scream. She yells mean things like, "Rotten child," and, "I can never trust you!"

How mean! I didn't do it on purpose, did I? The pastry is still in my mouth, but suddenly it isn't good anymore. I tell her, "Now it tastes like shit."

Uncle Otto has been sent to a camp in Poland. The camps there are not like here. There you have to work very hard. And if you can't work anymore they kill you.

They say that from now on there will be a transport to Poland every week. And suddenly everybody is very scared here in Mogilev.

[47]

A few days ago Mama said, "Marica, I have a surprise for you."

"What?" I asked.

"You can go to Palestine with the Red Cross."

"And what about you?"

"I can't go. It's only for children."

"How is that possible? Only for children?"

"Yes, for orphans. The Germans are making an exception for them."

"But I'm not an orphan! I have a mother! I have you."

She isn't going to make me go with those filthy children, is she? Those children behind the barbed wire over there. Their heads are shorn and they walk around in those ugly uniforms. Whenever I see them I always think, *How lucky I am that I'm not one of them!*

"Of course you're not an orphan, sweetheart. But what difference does that make? As long as you arrive safely in Palestine. Then Aunt Leila and Uncle Daniel can take care of you."

"And you . . . When are you coming?"

"As soon as possible."

"And if they send you on? Just like Uncle Otto?"

"Well, then . . ."

"Don't send me away! I'd sooner go with you to Poland!"

"Come on! Don't say such silly things." She shouted and started to cry.

But I didn't say silly things. I really meant it.

I want to stay with her, but she won't listen to me. And she even says that it is for my own good. But that isn't true. If that were so, Aunt Nina would send Bruno to Palestine too. But Bruno can stay here, with his own mother.

For two days she has been busy with my coat,

sewing the names and the addresses of all our family members into the lining. In case I need them. Ha! That's what she thinks! She also thinks that I am going—first to Bucharest, from there to Constanza, and from there to Palestine. Ha! At the gate I'll say, "I'm not an orphan. I have a mother. Look, she is standing right there!"

But I didn't say anything at the gate. I thought, *I'd better go. She doesn't want me to stay with her anyway.*

We've now been traveling for two days. The cattle car is so full that we can't sit down. Luckily I have a place near the wall. And there is a little crack between two boards through which I can look outside. As long as I can do that I don't have to look at the children. It is bad enough that I have to smell their stench and hear their cries.

It looks like the train is now slowing down. It is creaking and squeaking. Are we going to stop at last? Yes. Now we really are standing still.

Nothing is happening. We are just standing and standing. Now I hear footsteps and somebody unbolts the door. At last!

"Get out!" they shout. "You have ten minutes to eat and to pee."

When I'm finished I go back quickly because I want my old place back again. But I am not the first one in there. Another girl is there already. She is much older, she must be at least sixteen. She is holding a little baby in her lap, and she says, "Look at this—isn't he a darling? I found him lying in the ditch. I couldn't leave him there, could I?"

The other children climb into the car and the attendants shout, "Hurry! Hurry! We're leaving!" But just as they are closing the door the baby starts to cry.

The door opens again. An attendant asks, "Is there a baby in here?" Nobody says anything. It is dead quiet.

[49]

The only thing you can hear is the little noises the baby is making. Now she calls to the other attendants and climbs into the car. "Come here, you, with that baby," she says. The girl steps forward. She hugs the baby to her chest and looks at the attendant.

"Give me that child! You know very well that isn't allowed."

"No, I won't give him to you!" the girl shouts.

"Hurry up! That's an order."

The girl begins to cry. She begs, "Please . . . Can I keep him? I'll share my rations with him. He won't be any trouble to you."

"You still don't understand, do you, you stupid girl?" she yells and hits the girl so hard that she falls down. But the baby isn't even crying. He isn't hurt because the girl had wrapped herself around him before she fell. Now the other attendants join in. They grab the girl and drag her out of the car.

When the train drives off I can see her through my crack, walking away. And I watch her for a long time. She cradles the baby in her arms and her head is bent forward. She must have been doing that because she is singing him a song.

Suddenly I so much longed to be that little baby. He is very poor and has nothing at all. And yet he is so very, very lucky. Because he has that girl, who loves him so much.

The throbbing in my ear and the cut in my foot aren't even that bad. At least I don't have to be embarrassed about that. But that diarrhea . . . Whatever I eat, it comes out right away. I can't help it. I really can't keep it in.

Mrs. Niculescu is so nice. She says that I really shouldn't worry. My stomach is all upset. And she says that that is normal after two years in the camp.

She put my bed in front of the window, and I can look outside all day long. Sometimes the sun shines right into the room. Then everything suddenly changes color. And then everything seems beautiful again. Just like back then, way back then, when we were still in Csernovic. I have already been here in Birlad at Mr. and Mrs. Niculescu's three months. When the train arrived here they brought us to a shelter for the night. But when I saw those mattresses on the floor I started to cry because I did not want to stay with those horrible children any longer. The man who worked in that shelter came over to comfort me. That was Mr. Niculescu, and he said that if I liked I could sleep at his place that night. But when I woke up the next morning I had such an earache that they called the doctor. And he said that I was too sick to travel like that.

But tomorrow, I'm finally leaving to go to Uncle Dan and Aunt Anna. I've got a ride with a driver who has to take two German officers to Bucharest. In a real limousine! They musn't know that I am Jewish, of course, but who's going to tell them? Not me!

I don't like it all here at Uncle Dan and Aunt Anna's. And that son of theirs, that Axel, I can't stand him at all! He is spoiled like a little prince. He doesn't even go to school, his teachers come to the house. One for the languages, one for doing sums, and one for the piano. And on top of that a priest comes because they've had themselves baptized and now they are Catholic.

Aunt Anna has three rooms, all for herself alone: one for sleeping, one for doing her makeup, and one for her clothes. And then she even has a whole bathroom all to herself! I once counted her shoes—only the white ones—and she had twenty-four pairs of those! When I saw that, I had to think of Mama, who had exchanged all her things, up to her very last pair of shoes.

[51]

Aunt Anna did not come to the station. She was in bed with a migraine again. In the beginning I thought that that was a terrible disease. But the maid told me that that's what the rich call a headache.

In my compartment there is a couple who are also going to Palestine. I've told them that I traveled by train from Mogilev to Birlad and from there by limousine to Bucharest. They said, "You're quite brave, for a girl of seven." They kind of like me, I think. That's lucky, because we've still got a long way to go. And it's good if you have somebody to talk to on the way.

In Constanza the people of the Red Cross are waiting for us on the platform. They ask me my name and say that I have to go with the other children onto the boat. But I don't want to. I don't want to go on the boat with those orphans. Why do they keep sticking me with the orphans? I'm not an orphan!

Everybody else is already on board but I won't budge from my seat. A nurse walks up to me and says: "Come on, little girl. You don't have to be scared." "I'm not scared!" I shout. "I don't want to go on the boat with those children." She is very patient and explains to me that for children without parents there is no other possibility. But when I insist that I still don't want to, she gets up to get some help.

Here come two strong men . . . What shall I do now? I start to bawl loudly. And then suddenly I hear the lady from the train say, "The little girl can sleep with us in our cabin."

I have been living for two years now on the kibbutz. I feel really at home here with Aunt Leila and Uncle Daniel.

But I still keep having to think of those poor children. On the second night at sea, the boat with the orphans was torpedoed. And all the children drowned.

The boat I should have been on was sunk. And the boat I didn't belong on arrived safely in Palestine. Everybody thinks I'm such a clever girl because I was so smart. But I couldn't have known, could I? It was just bad luck for them. And it was just good luck for me.

I was lucky only because I was disobedient. If I had been a good girl I would also have been unlucky. And then I would have been dead. Just like the other children.

Today Marica says:

"Being sent away with those orphans was the most traumatic thing for me personally. My mother explained it all, that it was to save me and that it would be better where I was going. But even if I understood I couldn't help feeling rejected. And since then, things have never really worked out between my mother and me.

"I see the war as a negative experience only. I was only four when I learned the ugly side of human nature. There was no kindness and cooperation among the members of my family. What I saw was antagonism and grabbing and who gets what and more.

"I somehow decided that I wasn't a good person when I saw that girl giving up her life for the little baby she had found. I couldn't analyze it at that time, but I knew there were two choices: you stay alive or become a saint. And since I could not make that kind of a noble choice, I felt that I was bad. And later, when I heard that the boat on which I was supposed to be was torpedoed and that all the other children had drowned, this feeling got reinforced."

Camp Mogilev was liberated six months after Marica left. She and her mother emigrated to the United States, and Marica lives with her husband and son in New York.

PAVEL

Czechoslovakia

"Hello Mama," I said as I opened the gate. But she was bent so low over the tub that she didn't even look up. She just said, "Your dinner is on, Pavel. I'm coming in a minute."

I went to the stove and lifted the lid off the pan. Bean soup again. How silly of me to hope for something else. It was an ordinary weekday, after all.

Mama came in. She dried her arms and rolled down her sleeves. "I know what you are thinking," she said. "Just a little more patience, my boy. On Sunday I'll make poppyseed noodles for you and then you can eat until your belly bursts."

She filled my plate and put it before me on the table. The smell slapped me in the face. . . . Eat it quickly, that was the best thing to do. And think about something else. I shut my eyes tight and told myself that I had a plate with poppyseed noodles in front of me.

Somebody knocked at the door. It was the mailman, with a letter. Mama opened it hastily. I recognized the handwriting right away and knew that it was from

Tata.* Tata had been in the hospital for three long months, all the way in Bratislava. He had had an accident at work. Mama told me that a block of stone had fallen on him, but I didn't really believe it. Stone blocks don't simply fall on experienced men who work in the quarry. I knew that from Tata himself.

Once Mama took me along with her to the hospital. Tata was sitting up in bed with lots of pillows behind his back. Both of his legs were in plaster. And the color of his face was not brownish like before but all white.

"Hello, Pavel," he said and stuck out his hand. It felt moist and sticky on the inside.

"Come here," he said, and I knew that he wanted me to sit on the edge of his bed. My hand was still in his. He was holding it, but without any strength. I suddenly thought of those big strong hands I had always admired. There were two other men in the ward. But it was very quiet. The only thing I could hear was Mama crying softly on a chair behind me.

"How are you doing, Tata?" I asked.

"Very well, my boy. Especially now that I see you. You have grown again. . . . You will certainly be very tall, later."

Talking had made him tired. Under his chest hair I could see his ribs go up and down. For a second I thought that I even saw his heart beating.

"How nice that you came," he said. He let my hand go and sunk back into the pillows.

It was time to go. I stood up to say good-bye. As I bent forward he kissed my forehead. I thought that he had tears in his eyes, but I didn't dare look to see if it was really so.

*"Father" in Czech.

When Mama had read the letter she went to the stove to stoke the fire. Then she took the letter from the table and threw it into the flames. The only thing that I managed to read before that were the words at the bottom of the page. They were underlined twice and said, "Nobody should read this letter."

"What does Tata write?" I asked.

"That I should come and see him on Sunday."

"And about himself? How he is doing?"

"He writes that they have come and taken away Dr. Jezdinsky. You know, the doctor who took such good care of him."

"How come? Why?"

"Because he's Jewish."

She took a candle from the drawer and put it on the little table next to the statuette of the Virgin.

"What are you doing?" I asked.

"That one is for Dr. Jezdinsky. I'll light it tonight."

It was time to go to school. When I was standing at the door she said: "Here are three cents to get some yeast at Müller's on your way back. You won't forget?"

"No, Mama!"

That I surely wouldn't. If I had to get yeast, she must have some flour. And if she had flour, she was going to bake. I already saw her taking the fresh bread out of the oven. I knew the lovely smell that would spread through the house.

It was busy in the shop. Mr. Müller was serving Mrs. Vítek, Stěpán's mother. Stěpán was in my class. We used to be friends, but lately he wouldn't even look at me. He came to my place once and said that I didn't have a single toy that was worth owning.

The whole class was a little jealous of Stěpán because he was the only one who had real leather shoes. We all walked on clogs with canvas on the top. Once, when I asked Mama how Štěpán's father had managed to become so rich all of a sudden, she got mad and said: "It's all goods stolen from the Jews."

Mrs. Vítek was ready. She had ordered her groceries. And Mr. Müller promised that the errand boy would get it to her soon. As she walked to the door, he rushed past her in order to open it for her.

Once back behind the counter, he told the other customers what decent and kind people the Víteks were. He knew Mr. Vítek well from the weekly political meetings.

When my turn finally came, Mr. Müller didn't even bother to open his mouth. He just nodded his head for me to say what I wanted. I put my three cents on the speckled rubber mat and said, "A package of yeast, please."

He tossed it onto the counter right under my nose. When I stretched out my hand to take it, he hissed, "Just tell your mother she'd better come to the store soon."

"Yes, Mr. Müller, I'll tell her."

When I came home Mama asked, "Well? Did Mr. Müller say something?"

"Only if you would come to the store."

Without answering she went over to the shelf with the clock and took down the booklet that was lying next to it. It had a faded blue jacket, and long ago it had had "Müller's groceries" written on it in gold letters. She sighed and sat down at the table with it. I knew exactly what was going to happen next. First she would start leafing through the booklet. Then she would sit and stare into space for a long time, her head resting on her hands. And finally she'd start crying.

The best thing was not to be around. That's why I said, "I'll just go to the square, to see if the other boys are there."

The boys were trading stamps. I heard Zdenko say: "Not that one!" To which Stěpán answered, "But it's such a beautiful one." Zdenko shouted impatiently, "How many times do I have to tell you that I only want Czech stamps. Real Czech stamps, without Hitler on them!"

"I'm going to tell my father on you!" Stěpán shouted angrily. He was so furious that he got all red. The other boys laughed at him and shouted: "Mad Stěpán! Mad Stěpán! That's what you get when you walk around in Jews' clothes!" Stěpán became angrier still. He gathered up his stamps and screamed: "You just wait! I'm going to tell my father everything!" "Then you can also tell him that *we* don't walk around in Jews' clothes and that my mother is praying for the Jews!" I shouted after him.

When I came home Mama said, "Pavel, when I finish ironing, you have to help me carry the clean laundry to Mrs. Čemková." I always went with her when there was too much laundry to carry alone. But I also had a date with Janěk. After dark we were going to go and secretly eat cherries in old Kováček's orchard. So I said, "Okay, Mama. But on the way back I have to stop by at Janěk's."

"That late?"

"He wasn't in school today. And I promised the teacher to bring him his homework."

She mumbled something that I couldn't understand. But then she said, "As long as you see to it that you are back before dark."

Janěk was already waiting for me outside. Kováček didn't live far from Janěk's house, only about ten houses further on. But we'd never seen his house because his yard was surrounded by a very high hedge. That made us curious. We didn't talk on the way. Janěk must have been thinking about the cherries, as I was. I already saw myself sitting on a branch, high up in the tree. With one hand I'd pick the cherries and with the other I'd put them in my mouth, one after another, until I was so full that I couldn't swallow another one. And then I'd stuff my pockets full of cherries as well. And when I came home I would give those to Mama. How happy she would be! And she'd forget her anger completely.

We arrived at the hedge. Janĕk asked, "Shall I go first?"

"All right," I said.

He clicked his tongue and said, "When you hear me do this three times, you come too."

When we were inside you could still see the trees. They were a shade darker than the sky, but you could hardly tell one from the other. I thought, *We'll never find the cherry tree. It's much too dark already.*

Janĕk nudged me. "There! That's it, I bet!" he said.

If that was really it, then it was very near us. We only had to cross a small piece of grass. Janĕk crept in front of me, glancing left and right as if danger lurked everywhere.

When we were almost there, I heard something. Janĕk took one step back.

"Did you hear *that?*" he asked, scared.

"Yes! What was it?"

"I don't know. . . . An animal, maybe."

"Let's go back," I whispered.

I was scared. Everything seemed so creepy in the dark there.

Then I bumped into something. It was not a stump or a shrub. It was something . . . that was moving . . . that was alive. . . . And now it even made a sound— *Ooww . . . ow . . . ow . . .* —like a complaint or a moan.

Janĕk whispered, "I touched it! It's human . . . it's a child. . . ."

Again we heard: *"Ooww . . . ooww . . ."*

"Pavel!" Janěk hissed. "Give me your hand, here!"

I felt a leg and then an ankle and then a rope. . . .

"Is it tied up?" I asked with difficulty. My throat had suddenly become so dry that I could hardly speak.

"Yes! And the rope is tied to the tree!" Janěk shouted, his voice shaking.

"What shall we do?" I asked.

"I don't know," Janěk said. "But let's wait awhile. Maybe they'll come to fetch it soon."

We hid behind a bush. But nobody came. We had completely forgotten about the cherries. The only thing we could think about was trying to find out who could have left that child here.

We waited and waited. But nothing happened. Finally I said, "We have to go home. We can't stay here all night." Janěk was about to answer when we heard footsteps. They belonged to somebody who had come out of the house. Then we recognized the voice of the old Kováček. He said, "Come here, you dirty Jew."

We heard him doing something, and then he walked away. Back to the house.

"He must have taken the child with him," I said.

But then it came again, that moaning sound: *"Ooww . . . ooww . . . ooww . . ."*

We crept to the tree and blindly groped all around. Suddenly I held a leg in my hand. The rope was still tied around it. The old man had just shortened it. The child was now lying next to the tree.

"How could he! We must go to the police!" I cried— much too loud.

Janěk covered my mouth with his hand and whispered, "We have to be careful, Pavel. It is a Jewish child. . . ."

"But he is tied up. That's not allowed."

"I know that. But we still can't go to the police."

[61]

"Why not?"

"Because it's dangerous."

"How come?"

"When they find out that it's a Jewish child, they'll come and get him."

"But we have to do something! We can't leave him here just like that, can we?"

"Let's come back tomorrow. Now it's too late anyway."

"All right then."

"Pavel . . . Will you promise me something?"

"What?"

"That this will be our secret. Just between the two of us."

The next day I was in the schoolyard before Janĕk. "What happened to you?" I asked when he finally arrived. He was walking like an old, broken man. "My father beat me up," he sighed. "And I couldn't sleep all night. Not because of that, but because of the child."

Then I had been luckier. I got a box on the ear and was sent straight to bed. But I also slept badly because I kept feeling that *"Ooww . . . ooww . . . ooww . . ."* coming in waves through my whole body.

"Do you still want to go back, then?" I asked.

"Of course. We have to know if the child is still there."

The bell rang. Janĕk and I were not in the same class. He was nine and I was eight.

Quickly I asked, "What do we do then?"

"This afternoon I have to take the goat out, anyway. I'll stop by at your place."

The teacher said that we would have a visitor. Lieutenant Veselý, the leader of the Hlinkaguard*,

*Organization of Slovak Fascists.

[62]

wanted to talk to us. When he entered we all stood up. He looked at the class, cleared his throat, and said: "We have received complaints about this class. A few pupils have said insulting things about members of the Hlinkaguard. Such incidents are inadmissible and will be punished severely."

He paced up and down before the class. It was dead quiet; nobody dared to move. Suddenly he stopped and clicked his heels. He took a piece of paper from his pocket, looked at it, and asked, "Is there a certain Pavel here in this class?"

My heart beat in my throat and I said, "Yes, that's me."

"Oh, so I see." He looked at me from top to toe. Then he pulled a face and said, "So that's you. And, Pavel . . . Do you also have a family name? For instance your father's?"

"My father's name is Novák. Jan Novák."

"And where is Jan Novák? In the army?"

"My father is in the hospital. He had an accident."

"An accident! What a pity!"

He said it in a tone as if it were actually quite funny. There was giggling behind me.

"So, while your father is in the hospital, your mother is praying for the Jews. Did I understand that correctly?" The children thought it was funny. Drops of sweat trickled down my back.

"My mother prays for the people who suffer. And for those who are unhappy. And so for the Jews also."

He snorted and said: "Just tell your mother to go easy on her knees. Otherwise they may be worn out by the time she needs them for herself. So worn out that there'll be nothing left of them. Just like there'll be nothing left of the Jews, very soon."

Now the class burst out laughing. When there was silence again, he said in an almost friendly tone, "Pavel!

[63]

Why don't you join the Hlinkaguard? You'll get a beautiful uniform."

"But you have to pay for it yourself. My mother doesn't have the money."

"Then you'll have to wait until you earn some money yourself."

"The money I earn won't go into buying a uniform."

He got mad, shook his fist, and shouted: "You good-for-nothing! You'll never amount to anything! Soon you'll be walking around with a star, just like the Jews!"

He clicked his heels, said, "Heil Hitler," and stomped out of the classroom.

On the way home Zdenko caught up with me. "Don't take it too hard," he said. "That Vesely is the biggest bastard of all. My father said it himself."

"Really?"

"That crook knocked old Mr. Schwartz's teeth right out of his mouth."

"How come?"

"Because he didn't get up to say, 'Heil Hitler.' "

"But the old man is paralyzed. He can't get up."

"That's just it. That's why he's such a rat."

I started awake. Somebody was tapping at the window. I had fallen asleep with my head on my exercise book.

It was Janĕk. "Wait!" I called. "Let me help you with the goat." I went outside and we tied her up to a big nail.

We pretended to be doing our homework. But instead we were making plans for the evening. We were going to go to Kováček's garden before dark because we wanted to be able to see the child. At least, if he was still there. Mama stuck her head around the door and said: "Pavel, I'm just taking the laundry over to Mrs. Mednanska."

[64]

She had just walked out when we heard her scream. It sounded like a disaster.

We jumped up and ran outside. The clean wash was lying scattered all over the ground and the goat was drinking from the bucket. "Take that bucket away from him," she screamed. "There is chlorine in it!" Janĕk flew to his goat and pulled its head out of the bucket. And Mama went on moaning, her hands in the air, "Mother Maria! Good Heavens! Have Mercy!"

I stood there as if paralyzed. Everything that had happened these last few days came back to me. Only bad things were happening. . . . I ran up to Mama and shouted: "Forgive me! I thought we had tied the goat up so well!" I clung to her and burst into tears. Mama didn't say anything anymore, and after a while she began stroking my hair. When we had stood there for quite a long time, she said, "Just take the goat back. And better not say anything. Either it will die, or it will live."

On the way I said to Janĕk, to make him feel better: "Well . . . At least it's just a goat."

"I know . . . but I love my goat," he said, and then I saw that he too had been crying.

"Do you still want to go see the child?" I asked.

"Of course. We can't just abandon him."

Because it was still light out, we found the child immediately. It was a boy of about three. He was asleep. But we couldn't see his face because it was covered with his hand.

"What a stink," Janĕk said as he bent over him. I also smelled it, and then I saw that his legs were covered with dirty brown stains. He had done it in his pants. . . . Not once, but many times.

"Sssh . . ." hissed Janĕk. "Somebody's coming." He

[65]

grabbed my arm and didn't let go until we were sitting behind a bush.

It was Kováček's wife. She had a bowl in her hand and called, "Poldi! Poldi!" When she was at the child's side, she slapped the bowl down on the ground and shouted, "Dinner! Dinner! I have potatoes for you!"

The child woke up. When he saw the bowl he got up on all fours and threw himself onto it. His head inside the bowl, he started to eat and gobbled everything up down to the very last crumb. Like a famished dog. . . .

"Now drink!" she said when the bowl was empty, and she held a mug to his mouth. Poldi lifted his head and started to drink. He took such big gulps that we could hear the chug-chugging in our hiding place. The woman went back into the house.

I felt like saying something to Janĕk. But I didn't know what. I couldn't speak. What I had seen was so horrible that I didn't have words for it.

Janĕk was also silent. We just sat there, staring into space behind that bush. But suddenly, as if he came to his senses and remembered what we were there for, he said: "Let's go see him."

Poldi lay on his back. His eyes were open. They were big blue eyes, but they weren't seeing anything. He had a sweet little face, but it was covered with dirt and scabs. I said, "Poldi! Here we are again."

"We came back, Poldi. We are your friends," Janĕk said.

Poldi looked at us. At last. And then, again he did it: *"Ooww . . . ooww . . . ooww . . ."* I took out my handkerchief and started to wipe his face.

"You like that, don't you," I said.

"Ooww . . . ooww . . . ooww . . . ooww . . ." again. Now tears were rolling down his cheeks.

"Poldi," Janĕk said. "When we come back tomorrow, we'll bring you something nice to eat. Will you wait for us?"

"*Ooww . . . ooww . . . ooww . . .*" we heard again. But now it sounded different. As if he had understood us.

"We have to go!" I shouted. Somebody had rung the bell at the house. Janĕk had also heard it. He said in a rush, "Bye, Poldi! Be brave." And we ran to the hedge. Before I climbed over I glanced back. I thought I saw Poldi lift his hand just for a second.

I ran home as fast as I could. I only stopped once I got to the door. The whole world started whirling around me. I was so tired I just sank down on the steps. "What's the matter, Pavel? What are you doing here?" I heard Mama ask. She didn't say anything about my being so late. For a moment I thought she knew where I had been, and I decided to tell her everything. But then I remembered my pact with Janĕk. And I also realized that she couldn't do anything for Poldi either. It would only make her miserable. So I just said, "I think I'll go to bed right now."

"You don't want to eat anything?"

"Thanks, Mama. I had a plate of poppyseed noodles at Janĕk's."

"That's good. Sleep well, my boy. And don't worry about the laundry. It's hanging on the line to dry again."

From my bed I could hear her washing and undressing herself. They were familiar noises, and I was glad to be safe at home. When she started her evening prayer I got out of bed and knelt down next to her. She looked at me and I asked, "Mama, would you help me pray tonight for somebody?"

"Of course, Pavel. Who do you want us to pray for, then?"

"For Tata . . . and for a little Jewish boy who is very unhappy. . . ."

The next morning Mama said that I had slept very restlessly. I kept calling out, "Poldi! Poldi!" in my sleep.

Janĕk was not in school. When I stopped by on the way home his mother told me that he was sick. And she also said that she had found the goat dead that morning.

Janĕk woke up when I came in. His cheeks were bright red. I sat down, but after quite a while he still hadn't said a word. Maybe he didn't like it that I had come. So I said, "I should go. . . ." But then he whispered, "No, not now. Just wait a little longer."

There was a knock at the door and Janĕk's mother went to open it. When she'd left the room he pulled a bottle out from under the blankets. There were stewed pears in it. "Take it," he whispered. "My godmother gave it to me. I want you to take it to Poldi."

The bottle felt warm. As if it also had a fever. I quickly hid it under my coat. Then he said, "You can go now. And don't forget to take a spoon with you."

That evening, when I stood outside the hedge, I suddenly got a bad feeling inside. As if my heart was trapped in an iron vise. *Don't be a baby*, I kept telling myself. *You're only afraid because now you're alone.*

Poldi was lying on his back. One arm was stretched out and he held a bunch of grass. He had eaten some of it, but afterwards he had thrown up. His mouth was all covered with green.

"Poldi!" I cried, "You shouldn't eat grass! Look here, see what I brought you. . . ."

But he wouldn't listen. He didn't even move his head. He only stared at me with those big blue eyes. And then suddenly I felt that iron vise squeezing my

[68]

heart again. "Poldi . . . Poldi . . .," I begged. "Look here, look at these beautiful pears. . . ."

But nothing happened. Everything was just as quiet. The only thing that moved was a green fly walking over Poldi's chin.

I started to shake him. But he seemed made out of stone. "Please, come on now, Poldi, please!" I yelled.

The vise squeezed harder and harder. My whole chest ached. I dropped the bottle and ran toward the house. Old Kováček sat outside, on a bench. When he looked up I bawled, "Poldi! Poldi! He is *dead!*"

Today Pavel says:

"Despite the passage of time, I've never stopped seeing that little Poldi, that little Jewish boy who wanted to live, to live without fear, without being tied to a tree by the leg, without dying with a mouth full of bitter grass.

"What can I say about people like the Kováčeks, who promised Poldi's unfortunate parents that they would hide Poldi and save him from the gas chambers? Only that human cruelty is always waiting for an opportunity—it is waiting for that opportunity even now."

Pavel still lives in Nitra, the Slovak town where these events took place. He is married and works as a dental technician.

INGE

GERMANY

It's half past ten already and the sirens haven't gone off yet. Aren't they going to bomb us tonight? Or maybe they won't come till after midnight? I really can't stay awake that long. I've already fallen asleep once, or maybe even twice. It's awful to be woken up by those sirens when I'm fast asleep. Then I'm so tired I just can't get dressed. My arms and legs feel like they weigh a hundred pounds. And then, when I'm dressed, I have to rush, in the dark, quick-quick, down all those stairs.

But in our cellar it's always very nice. In the beginning I didn't know what was going to happen. Because before, when Vati* and Mutti** would talk about the neighbors, they would say things like "They're not our sort," or "We should keep the children away from them."

Mutti now seems to have forgotten all that. She chats with the neighbors as if she's always liked them a lot and as if she'd never said all that. I just hope that she doesn't mind my playing with the children next

*"Father" in German.
**"Mother" in German.

[71]

door all the time now. If Vati were here I could ask him. Or he'd say something about it himself. Because he's always so sure about everything.

I haven't seen Vati for months and months—a year at least—more than a year. When the telephone was still working he used to call often. He'd say, "Tonight we are going to the opera," or ". . . . to the concert," or ". . . to the theater." He has such a wonderful life there in Berlin. Mutti says that he goes all over the place with the Führer. That is his job.

Sometimes he sends presents. Once a green satin evening dress for Mutti with a matching fur stole dyed exactly the same color green. But where is she going to wear it? She never goes out. He's not planning to let her come to Berlin, is he? I hope not. On the little card that was with it, he'd written "Your Adolf . . ." How strange. That is his middle name, but he had never used it before.

For Christmas he sent me a porcelain ballerina. She has a pink tutu and makes a beautiful pirouette on her tiptoes. But unfortunately she is standing on top of a swastika. Such a delicate little doll on a big black swastika. They just don't seem to go together. How come Vati didn't see that? Wasn't that clear? But of course I didn't say anything about it, not even to Mutti.

Before, I thought that psalms were meant to be sung in the church only. But now I know that people go to church in order to learn them for when they really need them. The louder the noise of the bombs outside, the more beautifully we sing in the cellar. The other day, when the house next to ours was hit, the noise was terrifying. All that creaking and crashing coming from next door made me ache all over. The whole cellar was shaking and we all held our breath. But then suddenly— as if it had been planned—our voices melted together and a beautiful sound rose out of us as if it were coming out of one throat.

Mutti says it's been only three months since the bombing started. But that's not possible, they have been bombing us for years! Or at least one year. How else could she have changed so much in three months? She looks so stern now she's pulled back her beautiful hair. And her face is so pale. But of course I can't say that to her.

Mutti is terribly scared. She says that the bombs will fall on our house sooner or later. And then we'll be hurt, or maybe even killed. When she is so frightened I always snuggle up close to her. That helps, because then the shaking stops immediately. Often we sit like that for hours, clutching each other. Sometimes she starts kissing me and stroking my hair. And then she often says, "My little Inge, you are my very dearest girl. . . ." I never knew that she could be so sweet, so tender and so soft. How wonderful to have a mother who can cuddle with me like that. When I'm sitting so close to her I feel that she can protect me from anything. It's funny really that I never knew I had such a sweet mother. I'm not supposed to say it, not even think it, but I like the bombings. Because then I can cuddle up close to Mutti.

Poor Mutti. Being afraid of the bombs is one thing. But her biggest worry is that they will come for Karl and take him away. He just turned thirteen, and if they find him he will be sent to the front immediately. They don't make any exceptions. Vati being so important in Berlin doesn't seem to make any difference. "On the contrary," Mutti says, and then she starts to cry.

That's why she decided that we too should leave. The Red Cross is organizing transports to the East and the people said there already is peace over there. I wonder what peace looks like; I don't remember the time before the war. The only thing I can imagine going with peace is toy shops full of dolls and beautiful tiny clothes. And lovely cream cakes like éclairs.

Now that Mutti has made up her mind I don't mind leaving at all. The cellar is getting emptier and emptier. Most of the neighbors have already gone. Where have they gone? When they leave they don't say anything, they just look sad. According to Mutti, they don't know themselves. But they can't stay here, in the cellar. The whole city of Bonn is a heap of rubble. It is a miracle that our house is still standing. But the water mains have been destroyed, and there is nothing to eat anymore.

The peace in the East is not at all what we had expected. It has taken us a week to get here, but at long last we have arrived in Lansberg-an-der-Wachte. Mutti says that it is near the Polish border. The other morning we heard a strange rumbling from behind the hills. It got louder and louder and we thought it was cannons. In the evening the sky turned red. It was beautiful, but we couldn't enjoy it because we knew that danger was coming closer to us.

We were woken in the middle of the night last night. What was going on? Who were those people? Were they human? With those weird eyes? And those big, furry hats? They didn't speak. They only made loud sounds and chased us outside. Some people were so tired after the long trip that they couldn't get up and stayed lying down. Once they had got us to stand in a long line they went inside. And a few minutes later we heard shots.

Mutti is black and blue all over, and all scratched and cut too. I can't bear to look at it. We were walking along that muddy road through the fields when suddenly two of those soldiers came up to her. They grabbed her arms and dragged her away. When she told us not to stop and to go on, one of them gave her an enormous blow. He threw her into the ditch and then we heard terrible screaming. I felt all sick, as if my body was being torn open.

Karl said we had to go on. But I couldn't, my legs were trembling. Then he lifted me and carried me on his back. The noise got weaker and weaker, it did not sound like screaming anymore. Or was it only because by then we were too far away to hear it?

Since that day Mutti looks like a little old woman. She always wears a kerchief around her head. Fortunately not a black one, that would be even worse.

As we walk along I always look down at the ground. You never know. The other day I found a potato. I nibbled at it, very slowly. It was delicious. I never knew that raw potatoes could taste so good. And I never would have thought that you could just eat weeds and grass. But unfortunately they don't really help against the hunger. For a little while you feel filled up, but then your stomach starts grumbling just as badly again. How wonderful it must be, just for once, not to have to think of your stomach—to forget that you have one.

The other day a cow was mooing in a barn. They sent Mutti to milk her. And when she returned with a full bucket the soldier turned it upside down. I thought that was really mean. What have we done that he is punishing us for?

Sometimes we sleep in empty houses. But most of the time outside, under the stars. The other day I found a horse blanket in a barn. But somebody took it off me while I was sleeping. When I think of my little bed at home I just can't imagine that I ever slept in there. What a life I had, like a spoiled little princess! When I sneezed Mutti would say, "Oh, oh, Inge, let's hope you're not getting a cold again!"

I remember Mutti always made me drink chicken soup when I was sick. Without that there was no way, she said, for me to get better. Since we left home I haven't even sneezed once. That's just as well, because here we don't have any chicken soup.

I don't know which is worse, the hunger or my poor aching feet. I should have taken along those high shoes with the rubber soles. But when we left home it was summer and Mutti thought we were going to where there was peace. Since my sandals broke I have been wearing old rags tied around my feet. That is very hard to walk in, especially when it rains.

In the beginning I was very much afraid of the soldiers. But the Russians never harm children. Mutti says that I'm lucky that I'm only nine. That's why I always hang around, because you never know what you can get. The other day when they slaughtered a horse one of the soldiers threw the head at me. The thing was so heavy that it slipped out of my hands. But he even tied a rope around it for me and I could drag it to Mutti all by myself. How proud I was! Food for a week!

Mutti was very happy when she saw me arriving dragging that head. She thought I was a clever girl and said that I could take care of myself very well. But I didn't like it when she put it like that. Why is she so sure that I can get by all by myself? Does she think I don't need her anymore?

Once they made us stop for a few days. The women had to make new pants for the soldiers. For every pair of pants they sewed they got a slice of bread. When Mutti got hers she gave it to Karl.

Boys always come first. There's no getting around it, mothers love their sons more. It seems that it's always been that way. It's not just Mutti. All the German mothers are like that. It's normal, and I shouldn't blame her for it. That's why I wouldn't have minded a bit if she'd given me a smaller piece. A little less than half, like a third. Even, if necessary, a tiny little piece. But she didn't give me anything. None at all. And that I minded—a lot. So much so that I just can't forget it. That I hardly can forgive her for it. Does it mean that she doesn't love me at all? Or did she do it because she thinks I can take care of myself? But doesn't she understand that I do my very best only because I want to help her? Because I know that she is having such a hard time?

I can understand why she is so worried about Karl. Just the other day two soldiers came and took him away. He didn't even dare to look back to wave good-bye. That afternoon I couldn't find Mutti. She had disappeared too. But late the following night they came back together. Mutti didn't say a word. She didn't have to; I knew very well that she'd gone to the lieutenant and that she had slept with him. I can understand that. She sacrificed herself for her child. She is a heroine. But I can't tell her that of course. You can't talk about that kind of thing. What a pity, because those are the things that really matter!

The first time it snows we are walking through a village. School is just out and the children start throwing snowballs. I bend down because I want to make one too. But then I see my feet covered by bloodstained rags. I get a shock. What is going to happen next? Next, next . . . I don't want to think about it. I never think about the next day. I am just happy when the evening comes. That is the best time. Then I think, *How nice that I'm still alive.* Suddenly nothing else matters anymore.

Every night, before falling asleep, I give myself a little present. I make up a little story. Not just an ordinary story, but something really special. Something that doesn't have anything to do with ordinary life. Usually it is about a young prince who is handsome and rich. His life is perfect, only he is a bit lonely. That's why he always has himself driven around in his golden

[77]

carriage. One day, when he happens to pass by, he sees me lying there and orders his coachman to stop. He steps out, comes nearer, and slides his strong arms under my back. In a moment he lifts me carefully, as if I am very fragile. And while I am still asleep he carries me to the carriage.

In the beginning, in Lansberg-an-der-Wachte, there were more than three hundred of us. Now, after eight months, we are hardly a hundred and fifty. Of course we all know each other a little. Once I asked Mr. Schmidt where he thought all the others had gone.

"Most of them are dead. They died from hunger or they were shot because they couldn't walk anymore. A few have also fled."

"How did they do that?"

"They simply ran off."

"Is that why there was shooting last night in the middle of the night?"

"Yes, those two were unlucky. It was a brother and a sister. I knew them quite well. They left a letter for their relatives with me. In case they didn't make it."

"And you, don't you want to run away?"

"I am much too old and too tired. And nobody is waiting for me anymore. My wife died when our house was bombed."

"Do you know where they are taking us?"

"I suppose to one camp or another. And there they'll let us slowly starve to death."

A few days later I heard somebody whispering in the middle of the night, "Not now, idiot. There is a full moon."

"Can't you hear the Russians snoring? They're dead drunk. They had three bottles of vodka."

I saw two figures move and thought, *I have to follow them.* The only other thing I remember is that we walked endlessly. Until we saw a train that was standing still, and we climbed into it. I think I slept for a very long time, and when I woke up I was here in Berlin.

I've been here for three weeks now and my eczema is already a lot better. My feet still hurt a lot, especially my small toe. It is totally frostbitten and will probably have to be operated on. I only hope that they don't have to cut it off. But actually I'm not afraid of anything anymore. Nothing really bad can happen now that Mutti and Karl have also arrived in Berlin. The Red Cross told them where I was, and so they came looking for me here.

We have been back in Bonn a year, but we haven't heard anything yet from Vati. We don't even know if he is alive or dead. One evening, very late, somebody rings the bell. Could it be him? That's what we keep hoping, but it always turns out to be somebody else. That's why I don't even dare to think of his return.

Then we see a skinny man coming up the stairs. That can't be him—Vati is heavy and round. But it *is* him all right! Only there is nothing left of him! I can't believe it. My Vati has come back! It is a miracle! They had taken him to Russia and after one year they let him go.

That night I can't sleep. I am so happy and excited that I can only think of Vati. My prince didn't even come. Where is he? With him you never know. He is so sensitive and modest and prefers to stay in the background. But now I don't have time to think of him. I am much too busy making plans for our new life. At last we are together again!

Vati keeps on wearing his mess tin and mug on his belt and he doesn't want to eat out of anything else. He hardly ever says anything and most of the time he sits in the big chair, looking straight ahead. I tell him all kinds of stories about the bombing and about our long march through Poland. But it is as if he doesn't hear me. When I ask him what he did all that time he says that we could never understand. Only his friends know what he's gone through. And then he goes to the bar again and stays there endlessly, talking to his friends.

Once, when Mutti went there to fetch him, he got very angry. When they came home and the front door was shut, he started to hit her. Karl and I couldn't stand it and tried to separate them.

Since that time Mutti never goes to fetch him again. But when he comes home drunk he beats her up all the same. And he is stronger than the three of us together. Poor Mutti! I try to comfort her. When she is sad she seems so delicate and small. Then I throw my arms around her and let her cry on my shoulder. And we sit like that for a long time. Just like before, in the cellar. And then I am her little Inge again and I love her just as much as back then.

Today Inge says:

"I am not bitter. I think that people who have gone through so much suffering are somehow richer and that happiness and sadness affects them in a much stronger way. Emotions that spring from love, nature, music, and literature touch us deeper than those who have never been hurt or wounded. I also think that people who have suffered a great deal want their lives to make sense to themselves and to others. In a way I am even grateful for all that was decided for me."

Inge's father became an alcoholic and died shortly after the war. Inge lives with her husband and son in Hamburg, where she works as a librarian.

Jules

BELGIUM

"Papa! Papa! I want to go with you. Down to the corner."

"No question, Jules. You just go upstairs. Then you can help Maman with the beds."

"I don't want to go upstairs. I want to go down to the corner."

"Don't whine, Jules. I have to leave. I'm late already."

Now I start to cry very loudly. As if I'm hurt. Then he always listens.

"Come on. . . . What's the matter?"

"I don't want to stay home. I want to go with you. To the corner."

The other day the ice cream man was standing at the street corner. And I was allowed to go there all by myself. With twenty centimes in my hand. To buy myself an ice cream.

"But what is there for you at the corner?"

"I want to go look . . ."

"At what?"

"At the soldiers. I want to look at the soldiers. In Leopold Street."

[83]

"Why?"

"They're so beautiful."

"No way—you're not going, Jules. And stop it!"

I start to cry again.

"Why do you want to go to the corner? The soldiers march right by our house. Why should you wait for them there?"

"Because!"

" 'Because' is no good reason!"

Leopold Street is very long. You can see the soldiers when they are still very small. And then they get bigger and bigger. And suddenly they are close by. And at the corner they have to make a turn. That is so beautiful! And it goes so fast! And you can only see it there. There at the corner.

He is angry now. I start stamping my foot.

"I want to go down to the corner!"

"If you want to see the soldiers you just look out of the window."

The front door is already open. He is going outside. Try the garden. . . . Quickly!

"I don't want to stay inside. I want to be outside. In the garden!"

"All right then. You can go in the front garden. But I warn you! Stay inside the gate!"

I've been standing here a very long time. But nobody has come by. The soldiers must all be in Leopold Street. Maman shouts from upstairs, "Jules! Jules!"

Just let her shout.

"Jules! Jules! Jules!"

"Yeees. . . ."

"What are you doing there?"

"I'm watching."

"It's much too cold. It's raining, even!"

She comes out of the house. She wants to take me inside.

[84]

"I want to stay here! I want to wait!"

"For what?"

"The soldiers."

"Maybe they're not coming by today."

"Yes. They are."

"How can you know that?"

"I know it. They will come. They come every day."

Papa . . . Maman . . . It is dark. It is night. They say, "Come, darling. . . . Don't get scared. You don't have to worry." They tuck the blanket in around me. The big woolen blanket. I'm completely inside it. My head too. But I can still look outside.

Papa is carrying me. He is going down the stairs. We are walking down the street! Like that! I don't have to walk. He carries me all the way. Until we get to the underground shelter.

I love it when they come in the night, the planes that throw the bombs. Sometimes I can hear the bombs even before we get to the shelter. Then I see lots of little lights. It's so beautiful! Just like fireworks! And all that noise! So very loud!

The other day Papa lost his slipper. But he didn't stop. He left it lying in the street. He just ran faster to the shelter. And held me tight against his chest.

But in the cellar it's not so much fun. There Papa gives me to Maman. And I sit on her lap. Papa goes upstairs. And he stands talking with the other men and looking at the bombs. He can see them all. He can see them fall. And he sees the lights. I wish I was finally grown-up!

I passed the butcher's house with Maman. But I didn't see the bed. When the bomb fell on his house, the butcher was sleeping. And he fell down in his bed! Two floors!

[85]

If a bomb falls on our house I'll do what that old woman did. When she heard the noise she crept under the table. And after that the firemen came. She had slept under the table for three nights!

I hope the bomb comes soon. Maman doesn't like me to say that. She says that bombs are dangerous. And that they can kill people. Yesterday seven people died. But we don't even know them. And they live all the way in the Emma Street. That can't happen here.

This soldier here has something wrong with his foot. He can't stand up straight very well. He's wobbling a bit. Papa says that he can't fix it. If he touches it again the foot could break off. And then the soldier couldn't stand up at all anymore.

This soldier is naughty! He won't stand up straight! That's why he has to go to jail. To punish him. But then I won't have enough soldiers. Then I have only two short lines of four. If he isn't in jail, I have three lines. And that's much better. But he keeps wobbling! And that spoils everything!

Maman says that she can't buy me any more soldiers. There is a war on and they don't have any soldiers left. But I think she is telling lies. It isn't possible! Soldiers belong to wars, don't they? Like guns. And airplanes. And cannons. Maman is only saying that to tease me. Because it's my birthday soon. I'll be four.

Papa has counted them. There are twenty-seven of them. The soldiers that march by every day. The one that walks alone on the side is the boss. That is the chief. Papa says that he is a lieutenant. He walks so beautifully straight. All of them walk straight. But he walks even straighter. They march so beautifully in step: *tip, tap, tip, tap, tip, tap* . . . They march so well in time. They fling their legs up. All at the same time.

Completely straight. It is so nice to look at. And then, when they lower their legs, I suddenly see a tunnel. Could I slip through there very fast? I don't think so. It *should* be possible. But there wouldn't be enough time.

Papa also used to be a soldier, when he was young. He still has his cap. It is lying in the bottom of the wardrobe. The other day, when I heard the soldiers, I quickly went to fetch his cap. I put it on and went and stood outside on the front step. And when they passed by I held up my hand against it. And the lieutenant saw it. He looked at me and I saw his head moving! I shouted, "Maman, Maman! He saluted me! The lieutenant saluted me!"

But Maman was not happy at all. She doesn't like the soldiers. She never wants to come see them when they march.

I put Papa's cap back in the wardrobe. But I can't find it anymore. It's gone. Maman says she doesn't know where it is.

Where is he? What's become of him? Where is Jacques? He must be hiding behind that bush! But I can't call out to him. Otherwise they could hear us. And then they would come and look for us. If they find us here . . .

Here I am, all by myself. I didn't even want to come. Jacques wanted to go in. He's always got to see everything. He didn't even know what was here, before. He only knows because of me.

When I passed this way with Papa I asked him, "Papa, why is there always a soldier standing there? At the big gate?"

"He is standing guard."

"What does he have to guard?"

"The Gestapo."

"But isn't this the house of the Baroness?"

[87]

"Yes. Before. But not anymore. Now it belongs to the Germans."

"Papa? What do they do at the Gestapo?"

"That's a secret. They're a kind of police."

"Are they strict?"

"Yes. Very strict."

"Do they do bad things?"

"Yes. Sometimes they do very bad things."

"What kind of bad things?"

"That's not for little children. You don't have to know that."

"But I want to know! What *are* they doing?"

"They interrogate people."

"Which people?"

"People they suspect."

"What is 'suspect'?"

"When they think that people are against them."

"Do they suspect us? The Belgians?"

"Yes. Some Belgians."

"Papa! What is 'interrogate'?"

"That is when they ask things."

"And why is that bad?"

"When the people don't want to answer, they get a beating."

"Really? Grown-ups? And do they beat hard?"

"Yes. Very hard."

"So that they scream?"

"I suppose so. I don't know! Please stop it—stop asking all those questions!"

When I told Jacques, he wanted to go inside. He said that you might be able to hear the screaming in the garden. And then he found a hole in the hedge and sneaked inside. I couldn't let him go alone, could I? But I knew Jacques would be careful. He is much older than me. He is seven years old already.

When I came home Maman spanked me. Very hard.

[88]

But I didn't scream. I didn't say a word. She doesn't know where I've been.

Maman is sewing a big flag. Black, yellow, and red. The Belgian colors. Papa is not going to the office today, because it's a holiday. It's peace. The war is over.

Leopold Street is full of people. The Germans are leaving. The people say that they are happy that the Germans are going. And that they hate the Germans.

The Germans are marching, with the lieutenant at their side. But they don't have guns now. They march in step: *tip, tap, tip, tap* . . . Just the same as always. Very straight, without looking to the side. Neatly and exactly, in step.

The people are looking at the soldiers. They're not shouting nasty things. They could if they wanted to. They could even hit them. But they don't do anything. They're very quiet, all of a sudden. Are they still a little bit afraid? Or do they just like to see them march?

Here they are! The Americans! All the people are waving flags. They shout: "Welcome Yankees!" and they are very happy. The soldiers are driving open cars— "Jeeps," says Papa—and they're throwing little packages around. "Chewing gum," says Papa. It tastes good, but you're only supposed to chew it. You musn't eat it. The soldiers are waving their arms. They talk to the people and laugh. One is sitting and the other is standing. They've hung their jackets around their shoulders, and rolled back the sleeves of their shirts. And their caps! They're nice caps, but they're on completely crooked!

Are these men soldiers? Real soldiers? I'm sure they can't march. Certainly not as beautifully as the Germans.

[89]

Maman gets me out the door every morning at a quarter past eight. And school starts at half past eight. When I come home she always wants to know what we did at school. And then she wants to see my exercise book and my homework pad. And then she says, "When your homework is done you can go outside."

Before, when the war was on, everything was more fun. Then she never had the time to bother me. She was always busy with the stove. And she spent all afternoon in the kitchen. And in the evening, after dinner, I was allowed to play outside. Then she'd listen to the radio with Papa.

Now that I'm bigger I'm allowed to do much less. And nothing exciting really happens. There aren't any bombs falling, there isn't even ever an air raid alarm anymore. And you can't find anything good anymore, no shrapnel or cartridges. Not even empty cartridges. There is nothing left from the war.

Before I go to sleep I always think back for a moment to the war. To the time when the soldiers were in Hasselt, and marched past our house every day.

Today Jules says:

"I think of those years of the war as the happiest of my childhood. My family has never been as close as then, and the years that followed now seem drab. To me the war seemed like a big game, where some win and others lose. Until the age of thirteen I played violent games with my friends. We had great respect for militaristic values like discipline, force, and power. But when I was drafted I refused the military service and today I am a pacifist. I believe that playing war games and playing with arms are things that you have to do as a child. These things should be reserved for children and forbidden to adults. War is too serious a game to be left to adults. Only children are capable of avoiding excesses."

Jules is a family therapist and lives in Québec.

YURI

SOVIET UNION

Back then, back then, when we were in the country, at
the dacha . . . When we ate fish every day . . . Fried fish
with boiled potatoes . . . Hot potatoes with big clouds of
steam coming out . . .

When I take a deep breath I can smell those potatoes. And I can see that fish with the hard brown crust
and the soft white underneath. . . . Oh, that can't be
true. . . . I just can't stand to think about it. . . .

That deliciousness, that wonderful taste . . . was
that me? Or was it another Yuri who was eating that?

Mama says that we were still at the dacha this past
summer. So—it's not even that long ago. That's when
the war began. I didn't know a thing then. . . .

I remember the day the war broke out. Grandpa
had taken me with him to the post office. He had to talk
to Uncle Ivan in Moscow. In Gorodetz, you have to go to
the post office to make a phone call. But when we got
there, a lot of people were standing there. They were
waiting for the twelve o'clock news because Mr. Molotov
was going to say something. I didn't understand what
he was saying, but in Grandpa's face I saw that it was

something bad. When I asked Grandpa what was happening, he said, "The Germans have attacked us. And now it is war."

"Who are the Germans, Grandpa?"

"The Germans are our enemy."

"And are they strong?"

"Yes, Yuri, very strong. But not stronger than us."

"So then we're going to win!"

"Yes, we always win."

"But then war is not so bad, is it?"

"Yes, it is, Yuri. War is always bad. But a little boy of five cannot understand those things yet."

I didn't like it at all that Grandpa said that. But now I know that war is very different from what you think, and that it is always bad.

At first I went every day with Sasha to the Psovsy-way to look at the military trucks. The trucks rode in long lines to the border and they were packed with soldiers. I never knew there were so many trucks and so many soldiers in the world. Also, I had imagined the soldiers to be very different. I had imagined them laughing and singing. But they were very quiet. And when we waved at them they didn't even wave back. It was as if they were asleep with their eyes wide open.

After only four days, the trucks were coming back. In the beginning only a few, but then more and more. The same trucks, and the same soldiers. But their heads and their arms and legs were now bandaged. Not even with real bandages, but with dirty rags soaked in blood. And they weren't sitting upright, as before. They were sort of slumped over each other—as if they were lumps of bloody meat.

How long have I been lying here in bed, with all my clothes on? At times I think, *It's been years.* But a moment later it seems like just a few days. Maybe that's because there is hardly any difference between night and day.

At first, we would go to the cellar when there was an air raid alarm. But one day Papa said, "From now on, we will stay upstairs. All that running up and down is only making us weak." But that wasn't the worst thing. He also said, "The children are to stay in bed. All day. There will be no getting up or walking about. There will be no exceptions."

Grandma has come to live with us. Papa does not want her to stay in her own house. Her house is at the edge of our town, near the German lines. They are shooting all the time over there.

Mama is still unhappy that we stayed in Leningrad. We tried to get out just before the Germans shut us in completely. We went every day to the train station and we even slept there a few nights. But there weren't enough trains, and the people were pushing so hard that we could not get on.

I feel so strange. . . . "Mama, Mama!"

"What is it, Yuri? Why do you keep kicking the blanket off?" Mama is next to me and she pulls the blanket back over me.

"Don't, don't! I don't want a blanket!"

"But, Yuri, you will catch cold!"

"No, Mama, I'm terribly hot!"

I don't want a blanket, but she doesn't understand. Can't she understand then that it keeps slithering around, and that it's going to roll itself up, with me inside!

Mama says, "Come on, darling. . . . Take a sip of water and try to get some sleep."

I have slept a little and now I'm crying. But that doesn't matter, I don't mind that at all. Because when I

[95]

cry my face becomes all wet and I have to keep sniffing. After I've done that many times my mouth is full of snot and slime. And I like that because it tastes salty.

What are we going to eat tonight? We have already eaten our bread. Every day we get one piece of bread— one hundred grams each, exactly. The same amount for adults and for children. And that is our food for the whole day.

We are lucky because Grandma has a garden, and she goes there often. She has to walk very far through the deep snow. And it's very dangerous because the Germans shoot at anything that moves.

The other day, she came back with a bag of potatoes. They were frozen, but that didn't matter. They tasted so good. But the next time, she had nothing. Everything in the garden had been stolen. She was so angry she cried. She shouted, "If I ever get my hands on those thieves, I'll scratch their eyes out!"

Mama didn't cook anything today. Let's hope there is still a little soup left over from yesterday. I really hope so, because otherwise . . . otherwise, we'll just have to go to sleep again without anything to eat.

I think there is some potato soup left. I'm almost certain of it. There *must* be just a little left. The pan wasn't empty yesterday, it wasn't even nearly empty. That soup couldn't have just disappeared, could it have?

Later, when Papa dishes it out, I'll ask him to scoop some up from the bottom for me. Yesterday I got a portion from the top. And that tasted so watery, because on top the soup is always thinner.

The ceiling has beautiful curly patterns. If you stare at them for a long time they start to move. And then all of a sudden they seem to come alive. Sometimes they get very thin and long and they all start dancing with each other. Then I tell them to get short again but they don't take any notice of me.

Often they become even longer, and then suddenly they start attacking each other. Just like poisonous snakes. Then I shout, "Stop it! Stop it!" But they go on fighting. That's why I try not to look at the ceiling. I prefer to think about the time that Papa came home with a bag full of sugar. He had been given it at work, just like that—because families with children come first.

Oh, how delicious that was. . . . We got a teaspoon of sugar on our slice of bread. Every day, for at least two weeks.

How easy it all still was back then. I didn't mind at all having to wait all day for that slice of bread with sugar. Because that gave me something good to think about. What else could be better than thinking about a slice of bread with sugar?

But even then Papa was very strict. Our bread had to be cut in tiny little pieces. And they had to be eaten very slowly. We had to chew each piece a long time. But I didn't mind because that way it takes much longer to eat it. Only sometimes . . . sometimes, just once, I'd like to open my mouth very wide and just take a huge bite. One time, when Papa wasn't looking, I ate my soup very fast. But then I got cramps. The same cramps as when, before the war, I had an upset stomach. Luckily the cramps soon passed, but after that I felt terribly blown up. My stomach felt just like a balloon. And then—oh, how hungry I got all of a sudden.

Dmitri from next door is dead. It was just a few days ago that Papa got so mad at him. He walked in, without knocking. "Look here, here it is . . .," he said and pointed to a cookbook he was carrying. Papa shouted: "Stop it, Dmitri! Do stop reading all those

[97]

recipes. It will drive you mad!" But Dmitri pretended not to hear and walked to the table. He opened the book and said in a very strange voice, "Stir the butter into the eggs until the mixture starts foaming. . . ." Mama said, "Okay, Dmitri. We've heard it now. And please go back to your room." Then he began to cry and wailed, "But *look*, Olga! *Believe* me! There! There! There's the foam! I can smell it . . . I can taste it, really I can."

Papa walked up to Dmitri, put his hand on his shoulder, and pushed him out of the room.

And now they are talking about Dmitri. They don't know what they are going to do with him. Papa says that he still has the strength to drag Dmitri down the stairs and leave him in the street with the other bodies. But first he thinks we can keep him up here for at least ten days. It's so cold that it is freezing in here. And all that time we'll be able to use his food card. That will sure be nice.

In the closet, behind an old trunk, Mama found a bottle of cognac. It had been there for years, and nobody had remembered it.

I don't know what cognac is, but they are so cheerful. Tonight they have been drinking it in tiny glasses. First they poured the cognac into a thimble, and then into their glass. But when they finished that, Papa said at least twice more, "Let's have another round. Today we are celebrating."

Sasha and I also had some. A few drops in a glass of water. It didn't taste of anything. But after that I suddenly felt nice and warm.

Is it because of the cognac that they are suddenly talking so much? Papa says people are eating rats. *Brrr* . . . That must be horrible. But Mama says, "It's still better than dying from hunger." Who knows, maybe rats don't taste that bad. And Mama could make something delicious out of them, I'm sure. So you wouldn't even know that you were eating a rat. As long as you didn't think about that long, thin tail. . . .

We are lucky that Mama can make anything taste wonderful. Today we ate Papa's leather belt. First she soaked it for a very long time in water, and then she cut it into tiny little pieces. It was just like minced meat. That is—if I still remember well how minced meat tastes.

I've got my head buried under the pillow. But I can still hear everything. Papa is angry at Grandma again. He yells, "Mother! How many times do I have to tell you that you shouldn't drink so much water. You know very well that it's dangerous!"

"Oh, leave me alone—it fills me up. It helps the hunger. . . ."

"It doesn't do a thing! It makes you blow up like a balloon!"

"All right, all right . . . It does make me blow up. But it still helps. . . ."

"That's what comes from all that trekking to your garden—that's why you're so hungry."

Now Grandma starts to cry. I hate that. She says, "Please, Vladimir. Just leave me alone. I don't have to be around much longer. As long as you and the children can make it through . . ."

Papa is not so angry anymore. Whew! He gets up and takes out the bottle of cognac.

"If you're so thirsty, Mother, then take a sip of this."

"All right then, Vladimir. Let's drink together."

They empty their glasses in one gulp and Grandma says, "To tomorrow. . . ."

"And to all the other days," says Papa.

[99]

"But first to tomorrow. Because tomorrow, I'm going back to my garden."

Papa takes two books out of the bookcase. I know them, they are his favorite books. They are thick and are bound in leather. He says to Mama, "These I had saved for last. I had hoped to be able to keep them. . . ."

I am so impatient. I can hardly wait. When he goes to the black market he always comes home with such wonderful things. Once he had a piece of chocolate! Real chocolate . . . Mmmm . . . I'll never forget how that tasted. Every night before I go to sleep I think about it. Just for a moment. Because if you think about it too long, you start tasting it. And then you feel how it gets soft on your tongue. And how it starts melting. . . . But that's what I don't want to happen. Because it's so awful when you realize all of a sudden that you *don't* have anything in your mouth.

Papa's got a parcel. What could it be? Another piece of chocolate? No, that isn't it. He says, "There's hardly anything left on the black market. The only thing I could get was oatmeal." And then I hear him whispering to Mama, "Can you believe it, Olga . . . For a moment I thought that I could buy some meat. But Kouznetsov tapped me on the shoulder to warn me that it was human flesh."

This is our second winter in Levinka. We came here because we thought that there would be enough to eat in a small village like this. But that isn't true at all. I feel hungry more here than at home in Leningrad. There I lay in bed all day and I didn't know if I was asleep or awake. I'd stopped thinking about my stomach and I just felt as if I was floating.

The other day I suddenly had to cry. I missed Papa so much. He is still in Leningrad. But when I told Mama

[100]

I wished I'd stayed with him, she got mad and yelled, "Yuri! How can you say such a stupid thing?! We were nearly *dead!*"

"But there at least my belly left me alone. Here it's grumbling all the time."

"That's because there is still something in it. In Leningrad it was so empty that you didn't feel anything anymore."

"How come? Why does your stomach start to growl when you eat?"

"Because then it wakes up and starts asking for more."

"And when does it stop asking?"

"When you give it enough to eat."

So then, for the time being, my tummy won't leave me alone. Because all that we have left are blackened potatoes. The dandelions and the sorrel and the stinging nettles won't come back until spring.

Oh, I am so fed up with that growling in my stomach!

Last winter we still had the little goat. But in the end she too was hungry all the time, and she didn't give a drop of milk anymore.

If only the snow was gone, I could at least start searching for parsnips and turnips again. I know that there are all sorts of things under the ground. Oh, that parsnip I found last year! I stuffed myself. If I had taken it home Mama could have cooked it. Then it would have tasted even better. But then I would have had to share with the others.

Boris wasn't in school today and the teacher said that he would never come back. He had eaten grains of corn that had been lying under the snow. Poor Boris. . . . How could he have known that that made them poisonous?

Boris was always so terribly hungry. I remember

the day a group of us walked down the road a way. He pointed to the horizon and said, "Do you see, there, that dark line?" We saw a very thin line far away, so we said, "Yes!"

"Fine," he said. "Then you also see the forest. Because there, at *that* line the great forest begins, where everything grows . . . where you can find mushrooms, blackberries, raspberries, and strawberries."

"Hurrah!" we shouted, and we started to run in that direction. Only the forest did not come any closer, and after a while we were so tired we couldn't go on. We slumped down on the ground and asked Boris to tell us about the things that grew in the forest. He said, "The strawberries there are so big . . ." And he held his thumb and index finger at least two inches from each other.

"Oh!" we cried. And he said, "They taste so sweet . . . as sweet as honey. And if you bite into them they are just as soft as a breadroll."

We all sighed. I asked Boris, "When did you eat them?" But then he answered: "I haven't ever eaten any. My aunt told me about them."

When I came home I asked Grandpa if he would take me to that big forest sometime. But he said: "You silly boy. We are in the middle of the steppe. There are no forests here."

I have counted the potatoes, and now I'm sure that the grown-ups are eating in secret at night. That isn't fair. I would never have expected that of Grandpa and Grandma and Mama. Tonight, when they do it again, I'll go up to them and tell them it's not fair. Then they'll be ashamed, and of course they'll give me a little bit too. But they always wait so long before they begin. And it is very hard not to fall asleep first.

We are back in Leningrad. The war is over, but still I'm often hungry. Oh, how I would like to stuff myself so full that there wouldn't be room for a single bite! Maybe one day that could happen with regular food. But sugar—never. I could never, ever, have enough of sugar!

What I like best, the very best in the whole world, is chocolate. One day I got an American chocolate bar. It was first packed in silver foil and then once more in shiny paper.

I sometimes wonder how much chocolate they have in America. Could there be enough for everybody? And could there be children who eat chocolate every day? Surely not. That isn't possible.

Some time ago a group of German prisoners of war worked near our school. They had to dig holes and lay pipes underground. One day Alex was walking home with me. When we came to the prisoners he asked, "Whatever are you doing, Yuri? Why are you making such a big circle around them?" I pulled him along and said, "Watch out! Stay away from them!" Didn't Alex know what dangerous monsters the Germans were? But he pulled my arm and said, "Come on! Don't make a fool of yourself!" I was shaking all over and cried, "Careful! They'll grab us!" But Alex gave me a push and said, "Coward! Just look for yourself."

I looked and felt a shock. Not the shock I had expected. What I saw were not dangerous monsters but men who looked like skeletons. How hungry they were! Just as hungry as I had been. Suddenly I realized that Germans were also human. And from that moment on I couldn't hate them anymore.

But this morning we didn't see them. When we asked the teacher why, he said they had been sent to Siberia.

[103]

And now our class is being punished. We have to write an essay six pages long in which we have to explain why we hate the Germans and why those who give them food are betraying the Soviet Union.

I know exactly what I would like to write. But I can't, because then they would throw me out of school. What I would like to write is that I'm not sorry at all. That I am glad that for all those weeks I gave my school breakfast to the prisoners. And that I am happy that the other children did the same. I would also like to write that I had made some real friends. Some of them spoke a little Russian, and they told us about their wives and children back home. Germany is a very different sort of country, but still their stories reminded me of myself. And of our life before the war.

And once I'd written all that, I'd write about my friend Heinrich. He was only eighteen, but he made such beautiful things with his hands. He gave me a bow and arrow and I know that I'll never ever part from it.

Today Yuri says:

"I still feel that hunger is the most inhuman of human conditions. When your physical part is maimed, your spiritual part is dying too. It is very connected. When I see the Ethiopian children on TV, I understand them very well. They are passive. Passivity is the most exact word to explain my state of being at that time. Absence of any interest in anything except food. When there was food on the horizon, you just became a little bit more active.

"I get very upset when my daughter, who was born in America, starts to eat something and immediately throws it in the garbage. I understand that I am foolish, that it is another age, another world, another planet. . . . But nevertheless, I hate to see food not eaten.

"Suffering makes a genetically good person better and a genetically bad person worse. Personally, I am convinced that suffering from hunger, sickness, and the gulag have made me a better person in all aspects."

Yuri is a journalist. He has lived with his family in New York since 1976.

Yuri's story refers to the starvation winter of the siege of Leningrad (1941–42), during which half the population (two million adults and 200,000 children) starved to death.

CLAIRE

FRANCE

The needle was terribly thick and long, but I didn't even cry when the doctor gave me the shot. They put me down on a white table and Maman and Grandmère held me there. When the needle was in my bottom the doctor said, "Now we count slowly up to five." But he pulled it out when we got to four. In one hand he held the needle and with the other one he pinched my cheek. He looked at Maman and said, "Now our little Claire won't get typhoid."

Véronique didn't get a shot. She's still too little. She's only two. You'll see, she's sure to get typhoid, she always catches everything. And then Maman will have to sit by her bed all the time and I'll have to do all kinds of things for her. I'm never sick and now I'm not going to get typhoid either. But they say it's a terrible illness. Maybe you have it all your life. So then it's better this way after all.

When we came out of the Boulevard St. Martin we saw that the Place de la République was crowded with people.

"Maman, what are all those people doing there?"

"They're watching."

"What?"

"The Germans."

Maman and Grandmère had also stopped. There were so many people that you couldn't move. But nobody said a thing. It was quiet. You could see on the people's faces that they didn't like it at all.

"Maman? Is that them, there?"

"Shh . . . Yes. Quiet!"

How wonderful those men on motorcycles looked. They were sitting straight up and had beautiful suits. And those black boots . . . how they shone. They were happy because they were laughing and waving at the people. But the people only watched them, without doing a thing.

"Maman! Maman! Look over there! What are those things?"

"Shhh . . . Claire!"

"But what are they?"

"Tanks," she whispered.

"What?"

"Shhh!"

One of them was getting closer. How big it was, and what a noise it made! I felt the ground shake under my feet. There was a soldier up on top! I saw his head and his shoulders. And his fair hair. He laughed and waved at us. But look, there was the next one already! And the soldier on top was just as handsome. In a moment he would have passed by without seeing me standing there.

I would have loved to wave, just for a second. But I couldn't because nobody else was waving. But I wanted to . . . I had to . . . it was something I had to do! There must be something I was allowed! Why wasn't I ever allowed to do anything? Hey—he had nearly passed us already. . . . I could only see him from the side now. . . . The only thing I could still do was to stick my tongue out.

I felt Maman's hand against my mouth. She said: "If they catch you doing that they'll put us in prison!" Poor Maman, she's so dumb. She thinks that the grown-ups will be punished when the children do naughty things.

Maman is so different these days. She never laughs at my jokes anymore. And Madame Hirschfeld, I can't stand her at all. She comes over every day and never stops complaining. When I ask Maman why Madame Hirschfeld keeps on coming to our house all the time she gets angry. She says that we have to be nice to her because her husband has been taken to a camp.

When Papa was drafted, Maman was so worried that she cried all day long. She was afraid that he'd never come back. And when I said that everything would be all right, she wouldn't even listen.

One day I told her, just for fun, "You'll see, on Sunday Papa will return. . . ." And on Sunday morning, very early, somebody rang the bell. By that time, I'd completely forgotten that I'd said that. But it *was* Papa! He had run away and walked all the way back to Paris. I was so proud of myself and told Maman, "You see, I was right. But you never want to believe me."

Grandmère's bed is in the dining room now. Before, she used to sleep in the guest room. Now I'm not even allowed to go in there anymore. As if I didn't know about the big machine that prints those papers. Papa and Maman think that I don't see things. And that I can't keep secrets. I'm six years old now, but they still treat me like a baby.

Lucie and Pascale aren't allowed to come and play at our house anymore. Luckily it's summer and we can play outside all day. If only the war would be over before the winter.

[109]

Papa woke me up this morning.

"What is it? Where's Maman?"

"Maman and Grandmère left early this morning."

"Where to?"

"To the Midi. Paris is too dangerous for them."

"What about me?"

"For you it's not as dangerous. Nor for Véronique. Nor for me either."

"But why did they have to go?"

"You know that Maman is Jewish."

"Yes. But I'm a little bit Jewish too. Why couldn't I go with her?"

"Later, maybe. . . . First we have to see if they manage to get down to the South safely."

"And who's going to stay with me?"

"You'll be going to Courseulles-Sur-Mer. I found a nice children's retreat there."

"But I don't want to go there!"

"Come on, Claire. Don't whine. Lucky for you, you won't be on your own. Do you remember Marie-Ange?"

"That horrible girl . . . with red hair?"

"She's not horrible at all. She's very nice—you'll see. And she'll take care of you like a big sister."

How mean of Maman to leave like that, without saying a thing. But if she had told me I wouldn't have let her go. Of course, that's why she left without saying good-bye.

If only Papa was Jewish too, then at least we'd all be the same. And then we could all of us have traveled together to the South. But maybe it is difficult for five people to travel together. Who knows, maybe there'd have been no place to sit and we'd have had to stand all the way. Or we wouldn't have had anything to eat. But I think I wouldn't even have minded that. Not as long as all of us could have stayed together.

Oh, I hate them! I hate them all! The children and the Monsieurs and the Madames. They have a big garden here with swings and a big slide. But I couldn't care less. Lucie and Pascale and I used to play all day without swings or a slide.

And then that Marie-Ange . . . What a name for a nasty girl like that! When Papa comes for me I'll tell him everything. And then I'm sure he'll say, "Claire, you were right. I'd never have thought it of her." And then he'll surely tell her father. They know each other very well because he is also a typesetter.

I keep thinking all the time how to explain it to Papa. What it's like to be woken up by the bombs. It must be hard to imagine if you've never experienced it. I always find it hard to talk about things that are horrible. When I hear myself talking, I keep thinking, it wasn't *that bad*. But it was *that bad*, that's just it. Only I don't know how to say it.

So I woke up and it was pitch dark. I went over to Marie-Ange and I said, "I'm so scared . . . can I get into your bed?" And what do you think she did? She shoved me and said, "Get lost!" At first I thought she'd be sorry and say, "Oh, all right then, get in, Claire. . . . I was only joking." So I just crept under her bed. But she didn't say a thing and I kept waiting and waiting. It was so cold without a blanket and the floor was terribly hard. But the worst of all was that I didn't have anybody.

When I woke up I was all wet down there. I'd peed in my pants. But I'm not going to tell Papa that part. It will be bad enough when I tell him that it was terribly cold under the bed.

We're staying with Aunt Thérèse, me and Véronique. Aunt Thérèse is Papa's sister, but that doesn't

[111]

make her love me. I help her dry the dishes and I never leave my toys around. But she's never happy.

She never uses Maman's name, she just calls her "that Jewess." The way she says it, it sounds like something very bad. Something that I should be ashamed of.

There isn't even enough room at Aunt Thérèse's. That's why I have to sleep at the woman's next door. She's old and very ugly. But that isn't the worst. The worst is that she has a hump. A big hump on her back.

I can't stop thinking about that hump. And that rhyme keeps coming into my head. We always sang: "Crick-crack! If you touch the hump, it'll jump on your back!" It keeps buzzing through my head and it wakes me up at night. The first thing I do is to check if there is a hump on my back.

Aunt Thérèse won't let me go to school. She's afraid that people will ask questions. The only one I have here is Véronique. But she's far too little, she doesn't understand a thing. When I tell her how awful it is to sleep next to a hunchback it only makes her laugh. And she doesn't understand why I miss Maman so much, either. I think she likes it here at Aunt Thérèse's, because she's her little pet.

I just don't understand. If you don't like the Jews, then you should like the Germans, shouldn't you? Because the Germans hate the Jews. But Aunt Thérèse doesn't like the Germans either. Aunt Thérèse doesn't like anybody. Not even Papa. When she talks about him, she always says, "That stupid Communist. . . ."

The other day, Aunt Thérèse took us to the Bois de Vincennes. She had ironed our Sunday dresses and I had pink bows in my braids. There was a German soldier there who asked if he could come and sit next to us on the bench. He started talking to us and took me on his lap. And he said a lot of nice things about me being cute and smart. He showed us pictures of his wife and children. After Aunt Thérèse had seen them, he asked, "Don't you think that our little girls look a little bit alike?" Aunt Thérèse didn't answer, but he didn't seem to notice. He said, "It's so nice for me to be with children—I'd love to play with them again. If you don't mind we could meet again some other day. I am free every afternoon from three o'clock on. . . ."

When we left he kissed us both. And he also gave each of us a bar of chocolate and a box of candies. I didn't want to go home yet and kept waving at him for a long time. But once we were home Aunt Thérèse said with a mean voice, "Hand over that stuff." And she threw everything into the stove. What a waste! I can't stop thinking about my chocolate bar and my box of candies. A German had given them to us—but did that mean that we couldn't eat them?

It's Thursday. Will Monsieur Philippe come again today? He nearly always comes on Thursdays. I can't wait for Monsieur Philippe to come. He always brings a letter from Maman and money for Aunt Thérèse. Maman writes such lovely letters. She always writes that she misses me. And that she hopes we'll soon be together again.

The bell rings. It must be Monsieur Philippe! *No!* What a surprise! It is Papa! But he's so pale and skinny.

"Papa! Papa! What happened to you?"

Aunt Thérèse is shocked too. I can hear it in her voice. "Where have you been? My God!" she cries out.

"In prison. They kept me in for nine weeks. But they couldn't prove anything."

"Papa! Papa! I'm so happy!"

He says: "Claire, I have some news for you. Monsieur Philippe is picking you up tomorrow. And he's taking you to Lyons."

"What about Maman?"

[113]

"Maman and Grandmère are there already. And I'll be there in a few days if everything goes well."

"And Véronique?"

"Véronique will stay with Aunt Thérèse for the time being."

Monsieur Philippe is very rich. He has a lovely car. A big Citroën. They're sitting in the front, he and his wife (I think she is his wife). She's so pretty and so nice. I have the backseat all to myself. When I'm tired I can lie down on it, she said. What an idea! There's much too much to look at. Through the back window I see the trees along the road. The leaves are touching each other overhead and it's as if we were driving through a long green tunnel. There are not many cars on the road and we are in the most beautiful one of all. The trees must be thinking, *Here they come, the king and the queen with their little princess.*

I wish the trip would last forever. I'm having such a good time with Monsieur Philippe and his wife. We even ate in a restaurant, at a table with a white tablecloth. When you're with Monsieur Philippe you completely forget that there's a war on.

I'm with Maman again, at last! I am so happy. But Maman is very nervous. She smokes at least a hundred cigarettes a day. When Papa leaves for Grenoble you cannot even talk to her. She's so afraid that something is going to happen to him. I know that he has to go to Grenoble because of the newspaper. But if it's really so dangerous and if Maman hates it that much, why does he keep doing it?

I'm going to school again and now I'm already in fourth grade. Next week Maréchal Pétain* is coming to

*Head of the collaborationist Vichy government.

Lyons and somebody in our class is to present him with flowers. I wonder who the teacher is going to pick. Not Odile again, I hope? She already did it the other day, when the mayor's wife was here. Anyway, she isn't even pretty. It's only because she has those blond ringlets, like Shirley Temple.

If the teacher had any taste she'd pick me. I don't have ringlets but I do have blond hair, much blonder than Odile's. And the rest of me's much nicer. I don't say that aloud of course, but that's the way it is.

And I think it's fun to curtsy. It's not hard at all: You have to nod your head, bend your knees, and then hand over the flowers. I'm pretty good at it now. That's because I've been practicing, in front of the mirror.

When the Maréchal sees me, he's going to like me a lot. And once I've given him the flowers, he'll say, "Thank you, my child." And then maybe he'll ask, "What's your name?" I'll look him straight in the eye and say, "Claire, Monsieur le Maréchal." I can just picture it. Also the way he'll touch my hair very lightly when he's already turned away to talk to somebody else.

Maman got a terrible shock when I told her I was going to present the flowers to the Maréchal. She kept on saying, "Imagine, our Claire is going to offer flowers to Pétain! I don't believe it!" But she did go with Papa to the cinema to see the news. When they came home they said, "It was another girl! Thank God!" They were so relieved that they didn't even remember that I'd been telling stories. That was a pity, because I'd made up such a good excuse. I was going to say the teacher had chosen another girl at the last moment when she saw that my shoes were brown. That way maybe they'd buy me a pair of white shoes.

Papa shakes me awake. He whispers, "Shhh . . . it's a roundup . . ." He carries me to the big bed and I cuddle up to Maman. I feel her whole body shaking.

[115]

They're outside, carrying flashlights, and sometimes a beam of light comes in. The shutters are closed so they can't see us (I hope). We hear them come up the stairs and bang on the door. They shout: *"Aufmachen!"* but we don't move. We just stay in the bed, the three of us. I'm terribly afraid and I pray Grandmère doesn't open her door. She's all by herself in the apartment upstairs, poor thing.

It's getting lighter outside already and they are still going up and down the staircase. Papa sneaks to the window and looks through a crack in the shutters. He comes back and whispers, "There's a group of people out there. I can't see them. The only one I recognize is old Lodsky."

I'd fallen asleep. Mmm . . . how cozy it feels to lie so close to Maman. But she tells me to get up. Papa and Maman want me to go to school, just as if nothing had happened. After school I'm not allowed to go home but have to wait for someone I don't know to come and pick me up.

It's so quiet here, in the corridor. I don't dare go down. What if one of them is still down there? Papa and Maman said that nobody is going to harm a little girl. It's easy for them to say that.

I'd like to go upstairs. Just to see if Grandmère is still there. How can I go to school without knowing? But when I ring the bell she doesn't open the door. That's what she and Papa and Maman had decided among themselves.

I love it here, in Aiguebelette. The cows give us milk every day and the chickens lay eggs in their nests. We eat meat very often and on Sundays we have real crème caramel.

Madame Périssot says that the war is on here, too. But it's really hard to believe. We play all day long.

[116]

There's another girl too, her name is Jeanette. We often go and pick dandelions and feed them to the rabbits. When it rains we play in the barn. We have our own theater there, which we made ourselves with boards that were just lying around. And we also write our own plays: Jeanette let her husband go to the front. And now she's afraid he'll get killed because the enemy is much stronger. I'm the colonel on the enemy's side. When Jeanette comes to see me, I stand up straight. She's on her knees and looks up at me.

"Oh, mon Colonel . . . I'm so sorry . . ."

"About what?"

"That I let my husband go, Colonel."

"That you let your husband go where?"

"To the front, to fight."

"To fight whom?"

"I hardly dare tell, Colonel."

Now I'm losing my patience and I stamp my foot. "Confess! And be quick about it!"

Jeanette bursts out crying. "Oh, Colonel . . . You're the only one who can help me."

"Why should I help *you?* Stupid woman!"

"Because you are *good.* And the others are *bad.*"

"How do you know that?"

"I know. And I can see it. You are much *stronger* and much *smarter* . . . That's why you're also *better.*"

Now I take a deep breath and say: "You've been very silly. And now you're sorry. That's why I'll forgive you. You'll get your husband back."

Sometimes Jeanette wanted to be the colonel. But she played it very badly. So I told her that we should trade parts again.

Monsieur and Madame Périssot listen to the radio all the time. They say that the war is nearly over, it's only a question of a few more days. Madame Périssot is

[117]

very happy and says, "Just a little patience, girls, and then you can go home at last." And I'd hoped to stay here until at least the end of the summer.

Today Claire says:

"Once I had told my story I realized what an egoistic and spoiled little girl I had been. My parents were an extraordinary couple who went out of their way to save their children. With my mother being Jewish and my father working in the Resistance, printing an underground paper (the Communist paper L'Humanité) *they had to take terrible risks. But instead of acknowledging the stress under which they lived, I did silly things to attract their attention.*

"As a child you get used to the war. It kind of becomes normal. That is what is so terrible—or interesting—about children. They experience abnormal things and normalize them. In other words, what I lived was my childhood, not the war."

Claire has three grown sons and works as a children's dentist. She lives with her husband in Lyons, France.

ARJÉ

HOLLAND

"Arjé! Arjé!"

It's Mother. She's calling me. But I don't feel like answering.

"Arjé! Where are you?"

There she is again. As if I didn't know that Aunt Lea and Uncle Daan have arrived. It's Sunday morning and they always come for a cup of coffee.

I shout, "Just a moment! Let me finish reading *Brownie Bear!*"

Don't worry, I'm not going to stay all morning in my room. But I'm sure Father will be telling Uncle Daan the news right now. And I prefer not to be there for that.

Last night Father came to tuck me in. He never does that. Then he said, "I have to tell you something, Arjé. First something good and then something bad."

"What? Tell me, please!"

"Tomorrow afternoon we are going to the dunes. You and I."

He was silent for a moment. I saw him swallow. Now I really wanted to know. "And the bad news?"

"I have to turn it in on Monday morning—the motorcycle."

The bastards! For four years Father saved his money to buy himself a motorbike. He'd made a few trips with his friends. Once they went all the way to the Ardennes. And when the weather was nice he would take me to the dunes.

There is a knock at the door. It's Aunt Lea.

"Hello, my boy. I'm bringing you a piece of ginger-cake. You're so right to stay here and read *Brownie Bear*. We're only talking about sad things anyway."

Suddenly I have to cry. I don't know why. Not even because of the motorbike. But because of everything. And mostly because of the nice things. I love Aunt Lea so much. She lives nearby. Just like Grandma and Grandpa and Aunt Hester and Uncle David and Frits and Saartje. They all live here. I am never bored. When Mother is too busy in the shop I can always drop in on somebody.

"What's the matter with you, Arjé?"

"I don't know, Aunt Lea."

"Just tell me. Don't be shy."

"But it's nothing. I don't even know why I'm crying. It's just that I love you so much, you and Uncle Daan. And Father and Mother and Grandma and Grandpa and all the others. . . ."

"Is that why you're crying? Just because of that?"

"Yes!"

She gives me lots of kisses and I say to her, "Please don't leave. Don't leave, Aunt Lea. Stay with me forever."

She strokes my cheeks and my hair. She has such tender, soft hands. I don't dare to look at her because I am afraid she might also be crying. And then I'll start all over again.

"Aunt Lea?"

"Yes, sweetheart. What's the matter?"

"Can I ask you something?"

[122]

"Of course, my darling."

"Will you promise me that you'll never turn on the gas?"

"*What* do you mean by *that?*"

"I know that many people have done that."

"That's true. But don't worry, Arjé. We would never ever do a thing like that, Uncle Daan and I."

"You won't, will you? There—you promised!"

"Yes, my sweetheart. We don't think that's a very smart thing to do. You can't give up just like that. We feel the same way about those things as your father."

"And Uncle David and Aunt Hester?"

"Orthodox people think a little differently. They feel that you should always obey. But nobody in our family would do anything as stupid as turning on the gas."

Aunt Lea is right. Religious Jews are more obedient. The other day I saw that Grandpa's star is sewn onto his coat very neatly. Mine is only attached with a couple of loose stitches at the very tips. So if there is a sudden roundup I can rip it off like that.

Grandpa is sexton of the big synagogue. I go there every Saturday to help him. Father and Mother only go there on Yom Kippur. But Mother still cooks kosher because otherwise the family could never come and eat here.

Father doesn't like all that business about being kosher. Sometimes he's so fed up with it that he takes me with him to the Zeedijk. And there we have a great time eating smoked eel.

Father used to be a member of the Communist Party, so he's hated the Germans for a long time already. The first day of the war he said to me, "Arjé, remember one thing: the Germans can't be trusted. Just take care that they don't catch you."

One day last week, as I was leaving school at twelve,

[123]

I had to think of that again. The Germans had just held a big roundup and had taken the people to the Jonas Daniel Meijer Square. The people weren't allowed to stand up, but were made to crawl on their knees over the ground. It was such a terrible sight that I thought, *Father, you were right. I'll see to it that they never catch me.*

I've been sitting in front of the window with my roller skates on for hours. But now it is three-twenty-five. Another thirty-five minutes and I can go out on the street. Then I'll skate to the Alexander Boer Street. After school a bunch of kids always gather there and nobody ever asks any questions.

I've been at the Boersma's for two months now. They own a boarding house in the van Baerle Street and they have become my "Aunt" and "Uncle." My name now is Jantje van den Berg and I'm living here because my house in Rotterdam was bombed.

The other day a boy stopped me on the street. He wore a band with a swastika on his arm. He said, "We're having a party at the Concert Building. You're invited." I didn't have time to think and didn't know what to say in a hurry, so I just said, "I think I might be able to come." But of course I didn't want to at all. What would I be doing at a party with NSB*-ers? On the other hand, why not? After all, nobody knows who I am. And luckily it doesn't show that I'm Jewish. When I'm doing an errand for Mrs. Boersma they always want to know if everybody in our family has such lovely blond curls.

So I just went to that party. There were lots and lots of people. It was swarming with Nazi youth members. And they had the most wonderful things. Oranges, cookies, and real chocolate!

*Dutch Nazis.

At the exit you had to give your name and address. It took me by surprise, but I had no trouble quickly making up a false name and address.

Father and Mother are now in the van Baerle Street too. First they were in Arnhem, but it got too dangerous there. The other guests think that they are just ordinary boarders of the house. And I can't say "Father" and "Mother" to them because I live downstairs with the Boersmas. Of course, I go and see them often in their room. But I never stay very long because it's terribly stuffy in there. I don't know how they can stand to stay in that little room all day.

I can see in Mother's eyes that she cries very often. She says that she's applied for a new hiding place for Flipje. In Arnhem he happened to be in the same street as they were, one door down across the street. And Mother could watch him from behind the curtains, without his knowing it. Flipje was having a hard time. He was filthy and skinny. And she often saw him crying in the street.

What a shame that Flipje is only five. If only he were eight, like me, I'm sure he too could have come to the Boersmas.

We're all sitting together in the big room. Father, Mother, Mr. and Mrs. Boersma, and the other guests. Everybody is just sitting here, staring. Nobody says anything. It is dead quiet.

What's going to happen now? Are they coming for us? What are we waiting for?

The man they left behind says that they'll be coming back soon. He is sitting there so calmly, with his hat on. He doesn't even wear a uniform, just an ordinary raincoat. I bet he has a pistol in his inside pocket. Otherwise they wouldn't have left him alone with more than fifteen people.

[125]

Oh, it's taking so long! I can't stand waiting. And now I also have to go to pee, too. But I don't dare ask. It's getting worse. I can hardly keep it in. . . .

Why shouldn't I ask if I can quickly go to the toilet? He could always say no. But when I ask him, fortunately he says yes.

The corridor is empty and as I pass the stairs I look out into the street. Is there somebody standing out there as well? There must be. But what if there isn't. Why don't I just have a look and see . . .

The street is empty! I must try it. . . . It's now or never. Because if they take me away I'm lost. I'm sure of it. It's nearly dark already. Just before the curfew. Oh, and now I remember: Jansen, Johannes Vermeer Street 29. That's the nearest emergency address!

What a pity I couldn't stay there, at the emergency address. The very next day they took me here to stay with these people, in the Jordaan.* They are very strange people. When they talk to their children it's always something like "Shut up," or "Get lost," or "You idiot!" And that's when they're just talking. You should hear them when they're fighting. . . .

One time, they were going out. When she was standing in the door, she said, "I've put the string beans on. When the water boils, just put them in the bed." I didn't understand at all and asked, "Why in bed?" She snarled, "Oh, His Highness thinks we're scum, does he? But he'll just have to get used to it. Not everybody can afford an expensive cooking-box."**

I had no idea what boiling was. But when the lid had been making a noise for some time, I thought that must be it. And I put the pan in the bed.

*Old working-class neighborhood in Amsterdam.
**A box filled with hay that was used to save energy when cooking.

They'd hardly been back a minute when she said to him, "Go and get the string beans." And suddenly I hear him holler, "That bastard! Everything's burnt! The bed and the beans!"

He dragged me to the kitchen table and began to hit me with the carpet beater. He beat me and beat me. . . . And I screamed as hard as I could. But he didn't stop and just went on. For a very, very long time. So long, that in the end I didn't feel anything anymore.

The next day it hurt so much that I couldn't move. I was all stiff and black and blue all over. From head to toe, over my whole body. And all over you could see the round marks of the carpet beater.

And now here I am. All by myself in the attic. It must have been at least five weeks already. I don't even know if it was measles or diphtheria. But when I got the red spots and the fever, she said, "Go to the attic. If you stay downstairs you'll only give it to the girls."

Every morning a plate of porridge is put outside the door. And that's my food for the whole day. In the beginning I slept nearly all day, that made the time pass much faster.

Not too many walk through the Laurierdwars Street. Much less than a hundred a day. Yesterday there were eighty-seven and today, seventy-five. Tomorrow I'm going to count the bicycles and the cars as well.

It's in the evenings that I'm most bored. Then there isn't anybody outside. And you can't look inside anywhere either. Before, I liked to look inside because it was such a cozy sight. But now all the windows are blacked out.

When the family left for Maarn, and me with them, I thought, *It can't be worse than in the Laurierdwars Street.* But, what do you know! Here I don't even have a bed. I sleep in a chicken coop on a straw mattress.

And if I come home at night without any milk or cheese—watch out! Yesterday I biked all day without getting a thing anywhere. I was starving because I hadn't eaten anything all day except for that thin slice of bread at breakfast.

There was a bowl of pears on the table, but they didn't tell me to help myself. Before going to my shed I quickly snatched one. You should have seen the reaction! He unbuckled his belt, pulled down my pants, and put me across his knee. And then he started hitting away. Just because of that one measly pear! While the whole bowl was full! That was so mean that I've really had it with them.

Why should I stay with these people any longer? I'll run away. I won't live in hiding. I might just as well take care of myself. That's what I've been doing here, after all. All day, every day, pedaling into the wind. There isn't one farm between Wijk-bij-Duurstede and Bunnik where I haven't begged for food.

I wish I could see their faces when I don't come home tonight. They'll be furious that I took their bicycle! That'll show them.

Know what I'll do? I'll just ride over to that castle in Woudenberg. There they always give me food. I don't even have to ask for it. When they see me standing at the gate they already shout from the kitchen, "*Komm hier, Bursch! Du hast sicher Hunger.*"* The other day I got there around noon and the cook was sitting at the table with his mates. They said, "*Wir haben Bratwurst mit Kartoffeln,*"** and they gave me a plate piled high. It tasted wonderful. I hadn't eaten so well since home.

---

*"Come here, boy! You must surely be hungry."
**"We have fried sausages with potatoes."

It's nearly six o'clock. It's getting dark so early these days. I haven't found a place to sleep yet, and I'm so tired of that gnawing feeling in my stomach.

There are days that nothing works. Then I have to give myself courage. I tell myself over and over again: *Keep going, Arjé*, don't give up—you can't give up. I say Arjé, although my name is now Jantje van den Berg. But it only works if I talk to Arjé. Because isn't it Arjé who has to keep going, after all?

A little while ago I asked a farmer's wife who was milking a cow in the barn if I could sleep in the hay. Without looking up she snarled, "Get lost! Or I'll set the dog on you!"

But fortunately they're not all like that. Earlier this week I had a lucky break at another house. When I asked if I could sleep in their yard, they said, "That's fine. And you can also join us for dinner. Because we're celebrating a birthday."

There were also some other people. I thought that they might be in hiding, but of course you can't ask about a thing like that. I would so much have liked to know, because the woman reminded me terribly of Aunt Hester. She kept staring at me and when I looked back she got very shy. Then she smiled a little bit and I knew that in her thoughts she was far, far away.

Maybe it was because of that that I dreamed about Aunt Hester that night. I had no school because it was Wednesday afternoon and she'd bought us cakes. She asked: "Arjé, shall I sing you something?" and sat down at the piano. And she sang in a very lovely voice: "*Wien, Wien, nur Du allein . . .*"

What nonsense! Aunt Hester didn't even own a piano, and I remember that she can't sing. But the next day I kept thinking about that dream and I saw myself sitting in Aunt Hester's living room. And just that, the thought of it, was very nice. I knew very well that it was only a dream. But it was such a wonderful dream. Because just for a little, everything felt like before.

It is such an elegant house. And I think, *I'm going to ring the bell here.* But maybe it is too elegant. "Rich people are misers," Mother always said. But I still want to try it. A lady opens the door and says, "Hello, my boy . . ."

"Good afternoon, Madam. Please excuse me for ringing your bell just like that. I am Jantje van den Berg. I'm from Zeist. Our house was bombed and I have to get to Zwolle. My uncle lives there."

Why I say Zeist, I don't know. I don't even know if they have bombed that place. But it is true that I want to get to Zwolle. Not because I have an uncle there but because it is on the other side of the IJssel. And everybody says they have more to eat over there.

The lady says, "Well, why don't you come in, Jantje. Do you want a cup of tea? Or do you prefer a glass of lemonade?"

"Lemonade, please. If you have it. . . ."

When we are in the living room, she says, "Now, tell me exactly what happened."

"Well, our house was bombed. And then my parents and my little sister went to Zaandam. That's where my Grandma lives. And they sent me to Zwolle, to Father's brother."

"Don't worry, Jantje. We will help you."

"How kind of you. Thank you very much, Madam."

"Jantje, may I ask you if you have a religion?"

In the entrance I had seen a cross hanging on the wall. So I say, "I am a Catholic. But we don't do much about it."

"That doesn't matter. I just wanted to know because I wanted to discuss it with the priest."

"Thank you. That's very kind of you."

"Will you come upstairs with me? I'll show you where you'll be sleeping. Of course you haven't got any things with you."

"No, I haven't, Madam."

She opens a wardrobe and takes out some underwear and a pair of pants and a sweater. Then she says, "Here are some clean clothes. Would you like to wash yourself too?"

"Yes, please Madam."

When I come out of the bathroom she is sitting there waiting for me. She gives me a pair of shoes and says, "Try these, see if they fit you."

They are almost brand-new, with real rubber soles. I put them on and say, "They feel good on."

"You can keep them. And I also have a winter coat for you. That little coat you're wearing is much too thin."

"Thank you very much, Madam. . . . But I don't know I can accept all this."

She presses a finger to her mouth and I understand that I should say no more. Later, when the husband comes home, I hear that they had a little boy of ten. And he died just a few months ago.

Oh, I have such a good time here! What a pity I can't stay a little longer. This morning after breakfast, she says, "Jantje, it's all arranged. The priest has taken care of everything. Tomorrow you leave for Zwolle. The only thing left for me to do is to go to Zeist and see if I can find any of your papers there."

As soon as she is out of the house I take my bicycle and leave.

It's the coldest winter in a hundred years. That's what the people who stand in line to buy food from the farmers say. They also say that there is nothing to eat

[131]

in Amsterdam anymore. And that people are dropping dead in the streets from hunger.

I must, I absolutely *must* get to the other side of the IJssel. Once I'm there I'll go on north. The further north you get, the more there is to eat.

But when I finally get to the IJssel I don't know how to get to the other side. There are German soldiers standing at the entrance to the bridge. You can also cross the river in a small boat, but you need money for that. And of course I don't have any. So finally, after wondering for a long time what to do, I decide to take the risk.

I cross the bridge on foot, my bicycle along. Just like that, without looking to the right or the left. My heart is beating in my throat and my ears are buzzing. And it works, nobody stops me or asks me any questions! But when I finally arrive at Zwolle, just at the first houses, my bicycle snaps in two. And this time it can't be repaired anymore. So here I am in Zwolle with a broken bicycle and an air raid alert too. How am I going to find a roof over my head before the curfew?

A man who has taken shelter in the same doorway asks, "Are you from Zwolle?"

"No, from Rotterdam. I'm on my way north."

"Don't think that there's any food left there either."

"They can't have less than in the West."

"You're not going on tonight, are you?"

"No. Tomorrow morning."

"And where are you going to sleep?"

"I don't know yet."

"You can come with me, once the alert is over. I'll take you to Red Sien. On the Island."

"Is there an island here?"

"No, that's where the whores live in Zwolle. But don't worry about that."

He takes me to the old town, into a little shop that is still open. It is filled with German soldiers buying cigars and cigarettes. A tall red-haired woman is standing behind the counter. When she sees us, she says, "You can go straight upstairs."

She has a little room up there with a built-in kitchen, and we wait there until she finally closes the shop. When she comes upstairs she asks the man, "Is the boy looking for shelter?"

"You've guessed right again."

"There's always room in the attic. And this one can stay as long as he wants to."

That was in March, and Zwolle was liberated on the fourteenth of April. Everybody is elated and is celebrating. But all I can do is cry. I keep having to think of Father, Mother, Grandpa, Grandma, and all the others. I ask myself, *What am I doing here? I'm all alone . . .*

Red Sien tries to make me feel better. The war is finally over and we can start all over again. But when she says that, I just have to cry even more. Because what does it all matter, without my parents?

We've written to the Red Cross in Amsterdam. It's been four months. But we still haven't heard anything. Red Sien tells me that that doesn't mean a thing because the mail is still all mixed up. She means well, but nobody has to tell me anything. I know that I won't see Father and Mother again, ever. That evening in Amsterdam, when I walked out of the house in the van Baerle Street, I already knew that.

Today Arjé says:

"Looking back it seems incredible I was able to face those dangers. But I think that the solidity and warmth of my family background before the war gave me the strength to do it.

"I am glad I did not let the Germans drag me away. Children sense danger sooner than adults, and I have always felt that by running away I saved my life.

"Something that has stayed with me since the war is a certain distrust of other people. But in spite of everything, I am an optimist and still believe in the good side of human nature.

"I have to admit that the war also had its positive side, because it taught me to live more wisely. The people around me always make an incredible fuss when something bad happens. I agree that bad things are a nuisance. But I know there are things that are much worse. To me nothing really bad can happen anymore. Probably because the worst has already happened."

Arjé's entire family was exterminated. Only Flipje, his younger brother, survived. Arjé is a photographer and lives with his wife and three children in Amsterdam, Holland.

HILJA

ESTONIA

They could come for us any day, the Russians. Ema*
has heard we're on the list for deportation. She's thinking all the time about what she should pack to take
with us. As many warm clothes as possible of course,
because it's very cold in Siberia. You're not allowed to
take any precious things, but she's sewn her engage-
ment ring and her gold chain into the hem of her coat
all the same. She says jewels can sometimes save your
life.

　　To me it doesn't seem that bad at all to go to the
camp. They say it's very different there. So different
that you can't even imagine it if you haven't seen it for
yourself. I've heard that you only get food once a day
and you have to stand in line for hours. And for the
journey there they also have trains that are very different. Not coaches with compartments and benches, but
wooden boxcars like the ones they normally use for
animal transport. I've never been in one of those and
can't imagine what it looks like inside. I wonder if there
are any toilets in there. Certainly not. But then how do

*"Mother" in Estonian.

you go when you have to? It's a very long trip to Siberia. They say it takes at least a week. So they must have thought of something. I'd just like to know what.

The only thing that I'm afraid of is that they won't let me take Muki. I wouldn't like it at all in the camp without him because then I wouldn't have anybody to play with. No, without Muki I just couldn't do it. I've had him for so long. He's been my pet for five years. And when it's cold at night he always gets into bed with me.

Suppose I have to leave Muki behind. Who'll take care of him? And protect him? The war is just as dangerous for animals. People never think about that. They think only about themselves.

Ema and Isa* were afraid that they would take me to the camp too. That's why I'm now at Grandma and Grandpa's. To get out of town I had to dress up. I was wearing a skirt of Ema's that reached all the way down to the ground. And she gave me her black shawl to wrap around my head and shoulders. I really looked like a little old woman. Ema took me to the market and left me with the people who sell the potatoes. They're from the same village as Grandma and Grandpa and we have known them a very long time. When the market was over they took me along on the cart.

Grandma and Grandpa are very nice, but I'm so bored. There are no children to play with and nothing ever happens. The only thing I can do is read. But Grandpa's books are all so dull. There's just one that has a lot of pictures. It's a history book, about the time of Napoleon. But the pictures are all more or less the same—just men in uniforms covered in decorations and medals. And on their shoulders they have silly stiff

*"Father" in Estonian.

[136]

things that keep reminding me of the brushes at the end of broomsticks. But the men seem to like them a lot. They look terribly proud and I think they must all be very important in politics. Probably that's how I got those brushes and brooms confused with politics.

One day I was playing under the table. Grandpa didn't know. He had a visitor and they were talking. And suddenly I heard them talking about our brooms. Not just talking, but really arguing about them! At Grandma's they had two brooms. One for the inside and one for the outside. The one for the inside they used to sweep the rooms, and the one for the outside to sweep the steps and the hallway. The inside broom was old and worn out but it still swept pretty well. The outside one was new, but you could hardly use it because the stick was loose and wobbly. Grandpa had tried to fix it several times already, but it only helped for a little while.

Suddenly, Grandpa noticed that I was under the table. He said, "What are you doing there, Hilja? You want to discuss politics?"

I was a little scared of Grandpa, so I just smiled. But the guest said, "Maybe she does have an opinion. Go ahead, tell us what you think."

He was so serious. As if he really meant it. He had asked me to tell what I thought about our brooms. And if a grown-up asks you a question you have to answer.

"Our inside politics are old and worn out," I said, "but they still work all right. Our outside politics are new. But you can't use them because they keep wobbling all the time."

"What an intelligent child!" the guest shouted. "She's right! I fully agree with her!"

To which Grandpa said, "Leave the room, Hilja. You know you're not supposed to be around when I'm discussing with my guests."

[137]

I wondered why Grandpa sounded so angry. How could I have known the difference between broomsticks and politics? And what did it matter? I had been right, hadn't I? Grandpa couldn't possibly mind that the visitor had agreed with me and not with him? Somebody as old as him couldn't be so childish.

I am back in Tallinn with Ema. The Russians have deported Isa. They wanted to take Ema as well, but when she told them that she had a little girl they left her behind. What a relief! What would I have done otherwise?

Isa had to go in one of those cattle cars, and Ema went with him to the station. She told me all about it. But I'd rather have seen him off myself. Going to a camp is something very important. You aren't sure if you'll see each other ever again. Who knows, maybe it was the last time . . . I didn't even want to think about it. Still . . . I would so like to have given him one last kiss. Now I haven't even said good-bye.

But Ema said it is better this way. Because these things are much too sad for little children. As if I didn't know that. Of course it is very sad. But this way it is even sadder.

I didn't mind so much being hungry because then I can play the wedding game. Ema told me once what they'd eaten at her wedding. What a spread! To begin with, smoked salmon with toast and butter. After that bouillon with a very thin slice of lemon. And as a main course, schnitzels with peas and rice. And after that there was still the wedding cake! Three layers on top of each other, beautifully decorated.

When I was hungry I would line all those things up in a row, one neatly next to the other. I wouldn't start eating right away. First I'd look at them, taking my time, trying to decide which I should begin with. (The cake didn't count. That was separate and came much later.) The hardest choice was always between the salmon and the schnitzel. Actually I liked the salmon a little better than the schnitzel; that's why it was better to save it for after the schnitzel. But the salmon was the starter, so you were supposed to eat it first.

That's why I ended up taking turns. And whether it was the schnitzel first or the salmon, it made no difference: the moment I took that first bite . . . Oh, what a joy! My mouth was suddenly full of water and the taste flowed all over my tongue. I waited to swallow for as long as possible, because then I'd lose the taste. And I'd only swallow once I'd decided to take another bite. It was all my imagination of course, I knew that very well. But whenever I'd eaten like that I wasn't hungry anymore and my stomach felt completely full.

And then there was still the cake. What a treat! Now I didn't eat because I was hungry, but only because it was so good. But to cut such a cake is not as simple as it seems. Actually it's very complicated because there are so many possibilities. You can just go ahead and cut a slice from anywhere: from the top, the middle, or the bottom layer. But in a way that would be a pity because then it wouldn't look whole anymore. Maybe it was a better idea to lift the three layers off each other. Then you still had three different complete cakes. And then, if you wanted to have a piece, you only had to cut into one of them. I never was completely sure what to do. And once I'd finally made the decision, I still wasn't sure if I had chosen the best way. Sometimes I'd get so mixed up that my heart would start pounding. And then it would take a very long time before I could fall asleep.

He keeps coming back into my head, that man. I keep seeing him before me all the time. It makes no difference if I have my eyes closed or open. I try to chase him away: "Go, go, go away!" I keep telling him. But he's back again before I've finished saying it.

He's there since the day I played over at Helvi's and the air raid came. They kept dropping more and more bombs. It was much worse than usual and it wouldn't end. But I wanted to go home because Ema would be worried about me. When it was quiet for a few minutes, Helvi's mother said, "Hilja, if you want to go home, you should try it now. Please watch out and stay as close to the houses as possible."

As soon as I was outside it started again. It would have been better to stay at Helvi's. But it was too late, I didn't want to go back.

The Pärnustreet looked completely different. The houses were burning as if they were made of paper.* The tram tracks had sprung out of the pavement and were sticking high up into the air.

There was nobody else in the street, except for one man. I had seen him walking in front of me and now he started to run. I'll stay close behind him, I told myself. All of a sudden I heard an enormous bang. A bomb? I fell flat on my stomach and covered my head with my hands. After a while I stood up and looked for the man. But I couldn't see him. Only a little heap of stuff. But that was him. He was it. . . . There was hardly anything left of him. He had shrunk down to nearly nothing.

How could that be? It couldn't be, could it? Just moments ago he was an ordinary man and now he'd turned into this little heap. In just one second. . . . A little while ago he was still walking ahead of me. A little while ago he was still a human being. A human being who was breathing. And now he couldn't do anything

*In Tallinn the Germans used phosphorus bombs and many of the houses were made of wood.

anymore. Nothing was left of him. Just that horrible little heap.

When I got home we rushed to the big bomb shelter in the park. The bombing got worse and worse. Everything was shaking, everything was trembling. But I didn't care. I could only see that man.

Later, when we went to look at our house, we saw that there was nothing left. Only one wall was still standing, the rest was rubble with smoke coming out. It was very strange because it didn't feel like my house. But the weirdest thing of all was that I thought I'd already seen that smoking rubble before. Somewhere completely different. In another world or another life. But that wasn't possible, of course. It could only happen in a dream. I must have dreamt about it.

Once, when I asked Ema if Isa was still alive, she said she didn't know. That's just as well. That means there's still hope. He's been away for two years now and we've never heard a thing. If Ema had received some news she'd certainly have told me. I'm sure about that. Nearly completely sure. That's why I don't want to keep asking her all the time. It would make her feel bad because it would keep reminding her of Isa. And she thinks about him so much already. I know, because I do the same thing.

Sometimes I wonder what would have happened if they had taken her too. Or if she disappeared, all of a sudden. During a war, anything can happen. If something terrible happened to her, that would become of me? How would I get on? I am too little to earn money. If they asked me my age I could of course lie and say I was twelve instead of nine. But even then they'd say, "We are very sorry, but you're still too young."

The only thing I could do to earn some money would be to help behind the counter of one of those little shops at the movie theater. You can hardly call them real shops. They could easily let a child run them. They're just little stalls, with a few shelves to put things on. And the women they have standing in there are much too big. So big that you can't even see the sweets behind them on the shelves. Apart from that, I know much more about candy because I'm a child. I'd know exactly what the other children would like. And I'm also very good at adding and giving change and things, so I wouldn't have any trouble running the cash register.

In the mornings I could stay at home (since they only have picture shows in the afternoons and evenings) and take care of Muki. We'd only need one tiny little room. And I'd keep it very clean and tidy.

But whenever I've been thinking about my life on my own, I always feel bad about it afterwards. I feel ashamed because there's no reason to make that kind of plan. Ema is still with me, luckily, and she has promised never to leave me alone.

I feel so bad because everybody says that you have to love God. They say God is good and just. But that's not true at all. God is not good at all and He is not even just. That's why I can't love Him. It's a great shame. I really feel sorry about it. But I just can't help it. However hard I try, I cannot love Him.

The other day I heard a story. It was so terrible that I could hardly believe it. It was about Lodz, a town in Poland where there were many Jews. The Germans sent all those Jews to the camp. And as they were walking through the town with their suitcases, people started insulting them and beating them!

If God were good and just, He wouldn't allow that kind of thing to happen. He would do something to stop the deportations. But it seems as if He doesn't want to see those things.

Yesterday I spilled a little water on the piano. And five minutes later, when I tried to cut myself a piece of bread, the knife slipped and cut my finger. See, that kind of thing He doesn't miss. I think God wants to see only the small things.

We've been in Germany for three months now. Ema is working at the big aluminum plant here in Forchheim.

When we were back in Tallinn, I went looking for Muki every day in our old street. I kept on going there, but I never found him. One day I met the old lady who used to live above us on the second floor of our house. She told me she'd seen Muki. At least she thought it was him. She wasn't completely sure because he'd looked very skinny and was all covered in dirt.

So he was still alive, my darling Muki! I knew it! I'd always known! I knew he'd survive the bombs!

But when I called his name he wouldn't come. He was a little bit scared, naturally. I decided next time I'd bring him something good to eat. And then he'd come home with me. We didn't have much to eat but I was sure I'd find something. With me he'd never go hungry. He would soon feel at home again and start washing himself all day long. And then his fur would be beautifully shiny, like before.

I just couldn't understand where Muki could be. I'd gone there so often and I'd never seen him. Could the old lady have been wrong? When Ema told me we had to go to Germany, I cried and cried. I didn't want to leave Muki behind. But Ema was very nice. She hugged me and said Muki could come with us if I found him.

Finally, the day before we left, he came the very first time I called him. Muki! Muki! My darling! But how skinny he was. . . . And his fur was all dull and gray. . . . But who cared? He was still my own Muki.

[143]

I had a little pat of margarine with me and I let him lick it from my finger. Then he looked pleased, as if he hadn't eaten anything as good as that in a long, long time. And then he rubbed his head against my leg and I thought that I heard him purr, very softly. I stroked his back. But when I wanted to pick him up he sprang back. "Muki, Muki! Come here, come to Hilja," I cried. Then he came nearer, very slowly. He sniffed at my shoes and looked at me as if he recognized me. I bent down and picked him up, just like I'd always done. As I held him in my arms, I whispered in his ear: "Together again—at last!" But suddenly he slipped out of my hands. He ran away and disappeared into a crack between the stones. I waited until dark but he never came back.

Today Hilja says:

"The war has taught me that there are things you cannot control and have to take as they come. I know that every unpleasant situation will pass, one way or another. Therefore I am very rarely upset. Little things don't get me derailed. It has to be a major catastrophe to throw me out of focus. As long as I survive, it's all right. As an emotional experience, the war was positive for me, even though it had many negative aspects. It certainly made me a more balanced person and better able to cope with life.

"Another thing that has stayed with me is that I feel that nothing is totally good and nothing is totally bad. Nobody is totally bad and nobody is totally good. I'm not, neither are you. I must have sensed this from a very early age."

Hilja and her mother came to the United States in 1950, having lived for five years in a D.P. (Displaced Persons) camp in Germany. In 1957 the Red Cross informed them that her father had died in Siberia after one year of Soviet captivity. Hilja lives in New York, where she works as an ergotherapist.

FREDI

AUSTRIA

Another three nights of sleep and then it will be Sunday, and then we are going to the big arms show. All of us together: Vati, Mutti, Uncle Horst, Aunt Erika, and me. Liselore has to stay with Fräulein. She's only two and doesn't know anything about weapons.

I am already five years old and I know a lot about them. Not as much as Vati, of course, that would be impossible. Nobody knows as much as he does. Vati has even been to officers' school in Berlin. For nine months—and all that time he didn't come home. I didn't like that at all, but Mutti said that you have to make sacrifices for the Fatherland. When I asked her what "sacrifices" and "Fatherland" meant exactly, she explained it to me. It took very long, and I still don't understand it really. She also said something about security and protection. But I already knew that that was Vati's work. He was there to protect us. Us and all the other people in Austria and Germany.

When I grow up, I'll be able to play with the lead soldiers. Vati has a lot of them but they're behind a window on the shelf. They are very fragile, especially the old ones that belonged to Vati's grandpa. They are a hundred years old at least, because he was a captain in the army of Emperor Franz Josef. But they are very beautiful, and on some of them there is still a bit of real gold left. You can tell exactly what rank each one is, if you know them well at least. Vati has taught me all of them.

Sunday I'll wear my sailor suit and my new cap with the gold buttons. It really looks like Vati's. I can just imagine us walking with our caps on. Vati in his uniform, of course, and his shining boots.

Mutti is very proud of Vati. She often sighs, "So young and already a major!" Uncle Horst is thirty-two, and he is still only a lieutenant. But Aunt Erika doesn't mind. At least she doesn't say anything about it.

The arms show was even bigger than I had thought. There were many, many machineguns, thousands of hand grenades, long, long cannons, and even a real tank! Vati took me inside and he let me look through a tiny little window. But I couldn't see a thing, just some black stripes. He told me not to worry, even grown-ups found it difficult to look through a slit.

"But *you* can, can't you, Vati?"

"Yes. But I had to learn how."

"And are you going to drive in a tank like this?"

"Not right now. Maybe later."

"Then I'll go with you!"

He laughed and said, "Come on, Fredi. You're much too little!"

"That's exactly why! There isn't enough room for big people!"

I felt Vati's hand on my shoulder and he said, "War is not a game, Fredi. You still have a lot to learn."

As if I don't know that the war isn't a game. It is because of the war that Vati is never home. And now he is going all the way to Greece.

[148]

"Vati?"

"Yes, my boy?"

"Can't you stay a little longer?"

"No whining, Fredi. You knew that today would be our last day together."

"Yes, I know."

"Fredi, what do you want to be when you grow up?"

"A soldier, of course. Just like you. You know that!"

"If that's what you really want, Fredi, then you have to be brave, very brave. Starting now. You mustn't cry when I leave. And when you're sad you can't show it. Not even to Mutti. It's very difficult, I know. But do you think you can do that?"

"Yes, Vati. I can, I really can."

"You promise that you'll do it?"

"I promise, Vati."

Some people have yellow stars on their coats. When I asked Mutti why, she said, "They have to." And when I asked her why they had to, she said, "It is compulsory." I don't know that "compulsory" is, but she said it in such a voice that I didn't dare ask anymore. Maybe she doesn't really know herself. Or she just doesn't want to tell me the real reason.

The other day I saw an old woman with a yellow star. She had a dark coat on and walked with her head bent. You could see that she didn't want to be noticed. When we came close to her she stepped aside, to the very edge of the sidewalk. She did it very clumsily and I was afraid that she'd fall.

Nobody told me, but I know for sure that those people do not like to wear their star. Maybe it is a kind of punishment. I wonder why they would want to punish such a shy old lady. She couldn't have done anything bad, could she? But what kind of punishment is that? If you want to punish somebody, you should let him wear something ugly. Those yellow stars aren't ugly. They're quite nice. I don't think I'd mind so much if they made me wear a star like that.

My head still hurts a little because I fell. Mutti says I only got what I deserve. That's what happens when children try to race the elevator. And I had started off so well! The moment the elevator left our floor I started to run down the stairs. I was already on the mezzanine when it stopped on the second floor. But just then I bumped into two men carrying a big chest up the stairs. What happened after that I don't know, all I remember is a man's voice asking, "Do you see stars?" When I opened my eyes I was lying in his arms and I had to tell him which floor we lived on.

Mutti opened the door herself. The man clicked his heels and said, "Heil Hitler! Ma'am, here's your son. He fell down the stairs. But I don't think it's anything serious."

"Oh, my God! What happened? My darling, my little darling! I must call the doctor!"

"If you wish. But I could take a look at him—I am a doctor myself."

"Oh, that would be very kind of you, Captain."

". . . von Lenbach. Heil Hitler."

"I am Mrs. Goetsch. Anneliese Goetsch. Heil Hitler."

The captain drops in every day to see how I am doing. He says it's no trouble for him at all because he has a room at Mrs. Fischer's, on the second floor. Mutti is very grateful and gives him a cup of coffee. And then they talk about the war. They both agree that everything is going well. Hitler's army is so strong that nobody can beat it.

Yesterday the captain invited us to go to the mess hall with him. I could see that the other officers were jealous of him. They were all looking at Mutti and she was laughing happily. She looked very beautiful in her new coat. I didn't mind at all that the captain and Mutti were talking together. I could study the mess hall in peace. I had never seen so many splendid tables. And all those important officers. It was just like a party. They all looked terribly handsome in their black uniforms with those skulls on their collars. If you kept on looking at them those silvery skulls made you frightened. They weren't big or anything, they were actually quite small. But there was something about them. They made those uniforms look very different and much more beautiful.

Vati is back from Poland. He didn't like it there at all. There is no fighting going on, the soldiers just live in the town. Once when he was in the tram, a woman who had a baby in her belly accidentally got on the wrong car. In Warsaw the trams have separate cars for Germans. The ordinary people are not allowed to ride on them. A soldier pushed her off the tram while it was going. When Vati saw it happen, he immediately pulled the emergency brake and ordered a doctor to come and look at the woman and her baby. And after that he went right to the police station to report it. But the people there made fun of him, they said that it was normal and that things like that happened all the time.

Vati was happy when they sent him to the Eastern Front. We were allowed to see him get on the train, Liselore and I. But the station was very dark; there were no lights because of the bombings. Mutti was all pale and she cried hard when she had to say good-bye. And then, of course, Liselore started to whine as well. Only Vati and I were brave. When he kissed me he told me to take care of his women. That made me feel very proud.

[151]

I was shaking all over inside, but he couldn't have noticed that.

There was a telegram saying that Vati had been wounded. He had been taken to Silesia, and Mutti left immediately to see him. She wrote that he had lost his left leg when a grenade exploded nearby. But he was doing all right and she would stay in Silesia until they could come home together. I tried to imagine how Vati would look with only one leg. If he wore pants you wouldn't see it that much, it would look like he was limping. I hoped they would hurry up and give him an artificial leg. Maybe that's why they were still in Silesia. The telephone rang just as I was thinking about that. It was Mutti, and she said that Vati was dead. His wound got infected and he died within three days. I felt terrible, especially since I had been thinking all that time about an artificial leg.

Vati got a big funeral. But I couldn't be there because suddenly I got sick and had a fever. Afterwards they all came to our house, the family and the friends. They let me get out of bed and everybody was very nice. They pulled me onto their laps and weren't even afraid to catch my illness. Aunt Erika stroked my hair and said that I had grown again. When I said that I wanted to become as big as Vati she began to cry. Just like Mutti. I didn't like it at all that they cried like that in front of all those people.

Aunt Erika comes to see Mutti every day. I often hear them talk about Uncle Horst. Aunt Erika is terribly worried because she hasn't heard from him for nine weeks. Mrs. Rainer also visits us often. She is very sad. Mutti told me that her husband is in Russia. He has been taken prisoner.

I think very often of my dear Vati, and when Mutti goes to the cemetery I always go with her. Vati wasn't just an ordinary person, he was a real hero. He didn't die for nothing, he died because he was fighting the enemy.

Mutti often stays in her room with the curtains drawn. She says that she's tired, but that's not true because I can hear her crying. Nobody comes to visit us anymore because of the bombing. Everybody else is in the cellar, but Mutti prefers to stay upstairs. She doesn't want to be with all those other people.

From the kitchen window I can see the planes coming, hundreds at a time. They look like dots in the sky. And then, suddenly, they start dropping their bombs. Many, many, you can't count them, at least thousands of millions. They make the sky all gray, as if it had started to rain.

There's not so much bombing now, and Mrs. Rainer came to see us. She asked Mutti to go with her to the Gestapo. Mutti knows the commandant and maybe he can do something for her husband. We can come too because Mutti is afraid to leave us alone at home.

The commandant is sitting behind a big table, and Mutti and Mrs. Rainer are sitting in beautiful leather armchairs. They have been talking for a long time, but I don't understand a word of it. Then suddenly the commandant gets up and says, "I am very sorry, Mrs. Rainer. At this stage I cannot do any more for you. I'm just doing whatever I can to save my own people right now." As he was talking he laid his hand on his back pocket, where his pistol is. It is quiet for a moment. Then I hear him sigh. I see him giving a tap to his pistol and then he says, "And then . . ."

When we're outside I ask Mutti, "Is the commandant going to shoot himself?"

"Yes, I think so."

"Why?"

"Because we have lost the war."

"But that doesn't mean you have to die."

"No. But he prefers that to giving himself up."

"Is he afraid of the enemy?"

"That isn't it, Fredi. You are too young to understand these things."

I keep remembering that commandant and can't
forget the way he looked when he touched his pistol.

If he did it, he would become a hero. Then he would
get a big funeral and his family would be as proud of
him as we are of Vati. But I still feel sorry, because he
wasn't that old. It's nice to have a father who is a hero.
But it would be even nicer to have a father who is alive.

We were playing tag in the courtyard when suddenly a car drove in. An open car with four soldiers in
uniform, with guns. Were they the enemy? What were
they going to do? Would they start shooting at us, just
like that?

The people shouted from the windows: "Yankee!
Yankee! Welcome, Yankee!" When they heard that, the
men started throwing shiny little packages at us. We
ran up to them and they shouted, "Hello! Hello!" They
were very cheerful and I wasn't afraid at all. I was only
a little bit scared when I saw that one of them had a
black face and black hands. When he noticed how I was
looking at him he laughed, and then I saw that he had
beautiful white teeth. But they only stayed a few minutes. Then the courtyard was empty again. We ran
upstairs and Mutti said they were American soldiers
and that those packages were chewing gum.

In the evening somebody rang the bell. It was an
American soldier. He pointed at a package he was hold-
ing and said, "Rudi Hartmann." Vati had a cousin in
America with that name, so the package must be from

[154]

him. Mutti suddenly got all shy and didn't know what to do. Liselore started shouting that she wanted to open the package and pulled the soldier inside. He said that he was a friend of Uncle Rudi's and that we should just call him Joe. I had already noticed that he was a captain, but he said, "Don't worry. Just call me Joe."

Oh, the things that came out of that package! Chocolate, egg powder, soap, toothpaste, cigarettes, and nylon stockings! Mutti loved those things, but she didn't know what to say to Joe. But I think he didn't even notice. He put me and Liselore on his lap and made us laugh by pulling funny faces. When he left he gave us a few more packages and chewing gum and promised to come back soon.

Mutti and Aunt Erika are going on a trip with Joe. He is driving them to Mauthausen* in his own jeep. Joe has heard a lot about Mauthausen and he wants to see it for himself. It's a shame I can't go along, but he says that it really isn't for children.

They'll be home late because it's a long way. That's why Mrs. Fischer is coming to look after us. I don't mind staying home one day without Mutti. She never goes out anymore, and once she's back she'll have lots to tell.

It's half past six. I hear Mutti! I run up to her but she doesn't even see me. When I ask her how it was she walks straight into her room. She drops onto the bed and starts to cry. Mrs. Fischer goes after her and shuts the door in my face. When she finally comes outside again, she says, "Just leave your Mutti alone."

"What happened?"

"Nothing happened. She's just crying."

*Concentration camp near Vienna.

"About Vati?"

"No. Not at all."

"Is it because of Joe?"

"No. That isn't it at all."

"But what is it then?"

"She didn't like the trip."

"What didn't she like about it?"

"Mauthausen. She thought it was horrible."

"Really?"

"Yes."

"Is that all?"

"Yes. That's all."

"Is it true? There really isn't anything else?"

"No. Believe me."

"So she's only crying because of that?"

"Only because of that. Are you satisfied now?"

"Yes. I am."

Aunt Erika has been living with us for two years now. The Russians took her apartment away. There are two other families here as well. All together we are eight grown-ups and seven children. It's very busy and there is always something going on. The other day, when I told Mutti that I was happy being with so many people, she didn't answer. She just patted my head and said that I was a good boy.

Today Fredi says:

"My greatest regret is that I could never discuss these things with my parents. Shortly after the war, my mother died in an accident. I'll never stop reading about the war, trying to understand my parents' attitude, but without wanting to whitewash it.

"I feel that my sister and I did not suffer too much during the war. My biggest grief was the death of my father. But I think that it affected me mostly because it devastated my mother totally. I hadn't really grasped it, my father having always been someone very distant. I only saw him three weeks a year and to me he was mainly a hero.

"The experience of the war has determined my life. It has made me more serious. I realized this when I came to work in an international environment. My American and English colleagues had totally different reactions than I did. What they had experienced as problems during their youth seemed ridiculous to me. I found that I had much more in common with my Russian colleagues, especially with a few friends whose fathers had been officers in the Red Army, maybe because they had lived in a political system that was not so different from that of the Third Reich."

Fredi is a physicist and works and lives in Geneva, Switzerland. He and his wife have three adult children.

HANKA

POLAND

My dear Tatus*, he's changed so much. Suddenly he looks so small and pitiful. He sits there and cries all the time. I don't want him to cry! *He* shouldn't cry. Everybody else can cry, but not him.

Mamusia** is also so different. She doesn't do a thing anymore. There are clothes all over the place and the kitchen is full of dirty pots and plates.

The only thing Tatus and Mamusia talk about is death and dying. They say that the Germans are going to kill all the Jews. And we are Jews. But we aren't going to die! I know that they're not going to kill us. I know that. But when I tell Tatus, "You will see, you will see, we will live," he starts to cry even harder.

They sit there all day, Tatus and Mamusia. They are waiting because they know that something terrible is going to happen.

The bell rings. Tatus and Mamusia are frightened.

Luckily it is not the Germans. It is Stanislaw, a friend of Tatus. He loves him very much because when

*"Father" in Polish.
**"Mother" in Polish.

he was in an accident Tatus saved his life. Stanislaw says, "I have good news," and he whispers something to Tatus and Mamusia. When he leaves, he says, "Tomorrow morning at ten o'clock."

It is ten o'clock and a man comes. A strange man. He bends down and says to me, "Come along with me." *What?* Do I have to go with *him?* I don't even know that man! And I don't want to know him! He is bad. Bad because he wants to take me away from Tatus and Mamusia.

"Just come with me," he says, and he picks me up.

"No, no! I don't want to!" I yell.

I beat his head with my fists. But it doesn't help, he doesn't let me loose.

"Come on! And quiet about it!"

Be quiet? And go along with some stranger? I'll show you! I'll kick you . . . I'll scratch you . . .

"What do you think you're doing," he hollers and grabs my arms.

"I'm not going! I won't go!" I yell.

My legs are free, I can kick him. And with my teeth I bite his ear.

"I'm sorry, Dr. Lipschitz," he says in the end, and he puts me down.

He has left, the stranger. But I know it won't help anyway. I'm sure somebody else will come and take me along.

I am squatting here in the corner next to the piano. Tatus and Mamusia are standing in front of the mantelpiece. They're just standing there and they don't say a thing.

Why do I have to go away? Why can't I stay with Tatus and Mamusia? Don't they love me, then? They do. They say it all the time. But they also say that I'm a nuisance. And too little. But that's just it! That's exactly why I want to stay with them.

[160]

Tatus and Mamusia are still not saying anything. And I'm just sitting here, in my corner. They don't say why I have to go away. And I don't dare to ask them.

I'm just sitting here, all by myself. Completely alone. There are two of them, they have each other.

And now look. It's happening again. They're coming to get me. . . .

How big and fat they are, these two women! They have scarves on their heads, just like peasants.

They come and pick me up. I start yelling. But they're holding me so tight! I can't move at all. There is no way I can hit or kick them. The only thing I can do is scream and yell.

Tatus and Mamusia are still not saying a thing. Do they think it's all right? They aren't doing anything to stop them. They just stand there in front of the mantelpiece. They just stand there and cry.

I am looking at the trees outside. That's what I do all day. For many days. Sometimes I see Tatus or Mamusia. Only for a moment. Just a glimpse of them. All I can see is a bit of a hand or a leg or a wisp of hair.

I know that they can't come to me and that's why they play hide-and-seek behind the trees.

This isn't even a house. It's a hut. One of the two women lives here with her husband and daughter. But she isn't nice at all, the little girl. She's fat and dumb and never wants to play with me. Whenever I say something to her she runs up to her mother and hides under her apron. She's a real crybaby and yet she is already five years old. We're the same age; she's two months older, even.

The man is nearly always gone. He watches the forest, that is his job. He has a uniform and boots and a gun.

[161]

When he comes home he always brings dead animals. The other day he asked me to help him with the rabbits. He was holding them and I had to pull the skin off. It was dreadful. Those poor darling rabbits. They looked so terrible. All naked, without their little coats. I felt sick but I didn't want him to notice. I want them to think that I am brave, these people.

The first day the woman said, "Your father and your mother are dead and you are never going to see them again." She also said that I wasn't allowed to talk about my family or to mention anyone's name. Not even my own.

So I'm not Hanka anymore. Maybe it's better this way. Because Hanka was such a sweet little girl. She wouldn't be able to stand it here. Hanka couldn't sit here all day without talking to anybody. The woman never says a thing, she doesn't even talk to her own little girl. The only time I hear her is in the morning when she opens the grate of the stove. Then she looks into the ashes and shouts, "Oh, it's going to be a terrible day!" and says that the house is going to burn down or that the Germans are going to come and find me.

Tomorrow I can go outside for the first time. Up till now I wasn't allowed to go further than the back porch. Disgusting! It isn't even a real toilet, it's a stinking hole with crawling worms and dirty flies around it.

Look . . . look here at the moss under the tree. It's like green velvet. I remember our piano stool, how I liked to stroke it. But real moss is even more beautiful than velvet. It's much thicker and much softer. And in the forest there's so much of it!

Mmm . . . How nice it is to lie here on the soft moss. When I look up I can see the clouds. How big they are and white! It looks as if they're floating. No, not on water, just through the sky. How far away are they?

Very far, or not that far at all? I'd love to sit on top of that big cloud there. Then I could walk around up there and look behind all those hills.

Mmmm . . . What is it I feel? I know—it's the wind. It's started to blow. And it's everywhere. It is stroking me, I feel it even on my cheeks.

Look! Up there! What's *that*? I've never seen anything like it! It's like a curtain. A glittering curtain. A curtain made of gold! Is it real or am I dreaming? No, I'm not dreaming. I now see what it is. It is the wind making a curtain when it blows those tiny flowers from the tree.

Oh, what a shame. . . . The curtain has gone. The petals of the flowers are all lying on the ground. They are yellow and white, but you can hardly see them anymore. You only see the green of the grass.

I love the smell of the forest this morning. The pine needles smell so good when it's been raining. They are all clean and crisp and they crunch under your feet when you walk on them.

"Good morning!" I say to the mushrooms when I see that they have raised their heads up for me.

They like it when I pick them. Otherwise, they wouldn't let go of the ground so easily. I can eat them all day long. Only those that are pink and brown, of course. I'd never touch the poisonous ones.

But I like strawberries even more. There are lots and lots of them now; down near the stream they are growing in long rows. I'll go there in a little while. But first I'll peel a few pine branches. Under the brown crust they are all white and shiny. When they're clean I thread the strawberries on them and then I walk through the forest, looking for a nice place to eat them.

Where shall I sit today? Maybe on that big flat stone near the river. I like it there when it's been raining all night. Because the water is very wild then and makes a lot of noise. If you listen hard you hear voices—all kinds of voices mixed together. In the end they start calling you. I hear, *Hanka! Hanka!*

That's a pity, the sun is going down already. But I don't have to go back just yet. I can stay a little while longer.

On this side of the path the trees are very close to each other. Ordinary people can't even come here. But I can. I can go everywhere because I'm small and I know the way.

I love to play the tunnel game. Look, there's the opening! It's all dark inside and you have to run for a very long time. But at the end there's always a surprise: a beautiful flower or a special bird.

Oh, how long it is, this tunnel. I'd forgotten.

But there, now I'm getting to the end. I see a little spot of light and it grows bigger and bigger. I've got to keep running—just a little longer—and then I'll be out of the dark.

No flowers or birds this time . . . But oh, there is something much better! The whole field is filled with flowers—yellow, pink, white, and blue flowers. All those daisies . . . I've never seen that many. Know what I'm going to do? I'm going to make a daisy chain. But I can't. It's too late. I have to go home soon, and I can't wear it there. A beautiful daisy chain in such an ugly house. The flowers would die right away.

The light is still on. The man's brother is here, they are sitting at the table. He lives in Lesko, and when he comes he always gives news about the war.

"Hello my child," the man says and pats my head. How nice, he's never done that before.

The brother is leaving now and says to the man, "So you'll do it, as we agreed." The man doesn't answer. He pretends he hasn't heard. The brother gets mad and shouts, "Do you want them to kill *you*? *You* and your *wife*? Remember what happened to the poor Drewnows I told you about!" "But what do I do," the man whispers, "if her parents do return, after all?" "Don't worry about that!" the brother shouts and slams the door behind him.

The man is sitting at the table again. His plate is full but he tells the woman that he doesn't want to eat.

Go! Go! I have to go! I can't stay here! Quick, quick, into my bed . . . under the covers . . .

"Take this out to the chickens." It is the woman's voice. She's talking to her daughter, because she's the one who always takes the scraps outside. So it must be evening, that's when they feed the chickens.

What happened? Where was I all that time? Did I sleep all day? There is the wall and the window. The same wall and the same window. So I am in the same room. I *am here* . . . I *am alive* . . . So, he didn't do it. . . . He didn't . . .

But who knows, maybe they are trying to fool me. Maybe he is waiting for me in the room . . .

I have to find out! I have to find out! Now!

The man is not in the room. When I ask the woman if he is out, she says: "Yes."

Quick! Quick! To my forest!

As if I'm flying, my feet are so light. . . . I have no breath left. But who cares! I'm there.

Hello, my darling tree. There you are. You are always there. You are always waiting for me.

I am so happy to be with you again. It's here that I feel safe. Because you are the biggest and the strongest. Just look how thick you are. When I stretch out my arms as far as they will go, I still can't get them around

[165]

you. You'd need three children to do that. But I don't want that! Because you are mine, all mine.

You are not only the biggest and the strongest, but also the richest. No other tree has as many branches as you. And you even have branches that are thicker than the trunks of other trees! If I didn't have you, my dear tree . . . It's with you that I want to stay. Always, all my life.

Now what do I hear? There they go again. The whole bird family. What a stir . . . they're so excited. They're making a terrible racket. Why are they doing that? Oh, I know already! They are warning each other about the thunderstorm. The big birds are telling the little ones to look for a hiding place.

The lightning . . . Look there! How beautiful. . . . Ah! That was a loud bang. So loud that it made everything shake.

I don't have to look for a hiding place. I am safe under my tree. Here I won't get wet and I can watch the sky.

I hope the thunderstorm lasts a long time. And that the noise will get louder and louder. And that it will come sooner and sooner after the lightning. So that the sky is lit up all the time.

If only the snow would go down a little. I remember, last year, how dark it was. And how terribly long it lasted. And then one morning, a little light came inside. And the next morning there was a little more light. And the day after that there was a crack between the snow and the top of the window.

At last I could look outside again! But I still had to wait for a very long time until I could return to my forest. Because my shoes had already worn out back then.

Luckily for me, someone else came to stay in the

hut this winter too. It was a woman and she was very nice. One day she said, "Your hair is terribly dirty and greasy. I'll wash it for you."

She got some snow and let it melt. And then she heated it, specially for me. In the beginning I didn't like it at all because it hurt a lot. It took her so long to get rid of those knots! And when, at last, she could get through it with the comb she still had to catch all those lice. But after that I felt wonderful, so fresh and clean.

She looked like my Aunt Mania, the woman. I was sure it was her. When I told her that, she answered, "No, sweetheart, my name is Poniatowka." Aunt Mania had a gold tooth on the side of her mouth. And the woman had a hole in exactly the same place. But when I said, "My Aunt Mania had a gold tooth there," she said, "Isn't that strange? But I'm really not your aunt. I am Poniatowka."

Once I woke up in the middle of the night. She was lying next to me and crying. I asked, "What's the matter? Why are you crying?" She said, "Don't worry about me, darling," and went on crying.

I still don't understand that. Why did she come over and cry so close to me if she wasn't my Aunt Mania after all?

It's the first day I've been outside. The sun is really warm now. Oh, look at those streaks of water at the side of the path. They're just like tiny little rivers! They were just born right now, those rivers. Before that they didn't exist. Before that they were snow. They make all kinds of trickling noises. How sweet, it's as if they're singing a song.

What's that, down there on the road? German soldiers? Quick! Quick! I have to hide! Luckily I'm near to the house and I can run to my hiding place.

I hear: *Hanka! Hanka!* Who's that? Nobody knows

[167]

my name. What can it be? I'm not moving out, I'm staying right here, safe.

Hanka! Hanka! I hear again, *It's me, your Mamusia!*

Tatus has been standing in line all day long. He was at the IRO* and they said we can't get a visa for Palestine here in Bucharest. We should have asked for it back in Budapest. But at that time the IRO did not have an office in Budapest.

We have been on the road for nearly a year, staying in lots of different places. We stay in one place until they tell us that they can't do anything for us and then we go on.

Aunt Cipi and Aunt Rochal and Uncle Mordechai are also going to Palestine. They have been in concentration camps and never stop talking about the horrible things they saw there. We're always with them and I can't stand those stories about the roll calls, the kapos, and the gas chambers anymore.

Tatus and Mamusia are just as nice as before. But they're very thin and pale because they spent all that time in a hole under Stanislaw's workshop, without any heat, and there wasn't even enough space to stretch their legs.

How lucky I was! I had such a lovely time in my forest. It was great, it was marvelous there. I wish I could hug my big tree once more again. . . .

*International Refugee Organization.

Today Hanka says:

"After the war I lived in a fog, and until I got into therapy I couldn't deal with my feelings.

"What happened, in fact, was that I retreated from reality into the forest. The conditions were so extreme that I escaped into fantasy. I must have used a part of the mind that certain mystics can discipline themselves to enter. Today I wouldn't be able to let go of my senses like that. But as a child of four or five you have extraordinary powers to fool yourself.

"I think those were the most intense years of my life. It was an immediate, 'right now' existence, living day-to-day, alone with nature. I was so happy in that forest, I'd like to be able to recapture that. If I could be born a second time and able to record it better, I'd like to go through it again. I see it as a terrific loss, as if I have been thrown out of Paradise."

Hanka is a painter. She lives with her husband and two sons in New York.

ANDRÉ

SWITZERLAND

"Maman! Maman!"

"What's the matter, André? What *are* you doing?"

I'd stuck my head under her apron and pressed it against her belly. That always worked.

"Maman, you have to come. . . ."

"Where to?"

"To the garden."

"Come on, you don't need me for that. You can do that by yourself."

"But you have to come and look."

"At what?"

"At me on the swing. I can go very high. As high as Cécile."

With my back against the seat I pushed it up as high as I could, and when it fell I quickly jumped on it. When it came down I gave myself a push with my feet again. Suddenly I took off and flew up into the sky. All the way up! It went through my whole body, but it wasn't really scary. It was wonderful. Maman hadn't even seen me do it yet. She must have thought I'd never learn.

"I've only two more apples to do," she said, "then

I'll come and watch you—as soon as I've put the tart in the oven."

It would have been nicer if she'd come right away. Then we'd walk together right over to the other end of the garden, to the cherry tree with the swing. But she wanted me to go ahead without her. I could do that, too. Then she'd see on her way how beautifully I could fly.

It worked—again. This time it was even better. I hardly had to push myself off. I didn't even know how I did it. It went all by itself. I was already high, high up. But where *was* she? Wasn't she going to come right away? I always got a little scared if she left me alone for long. But why *should* I be afraid? It was going well, wasn't it? And it was fun. I knew how to have fun by myself. Just like Cécile.

Oh, no . . . Not now . . . Please . . . There they are again, the sirens. . . . That awful noise!

Here I am, on the swing, all by myself. I can't move my arms, either one. If I let go of the ropes I'll fall down. I've got to stop! Quick! Quick! Otherwise I'll still be here when they come. All alone by myself!

"André! André! What's the matter with you? You know when there is an air raid you must come in at once!"

She lifted me off the swing and took me inside.

"Come on—what are those tears for now?"

I couldn't tell her that, she wouldn't understand anyway. The other day I told her I'd seen the Germans close by, at night. And she hadn't believed me. She said it was nonsense because there were no Germans in Switzerland. There is no war here, she said. I didn't have to worry about that.

But that's all she said. Because she doesn't want me to be afraid. But I know it isn't true. Why would János be eating at our place, otherwise? Every Tuesday and every Thursday? He ran away from the Germans. All the way from Hungary. They wanted to kill him because he was Jewish. He told me that himself.

I don't know exactly what "Jewish" is. But János doesn't seem to be anything special. He looks exactly the same way we do. He even looks a little bit like Eric, my big cousin. I can't see the difference. So maybe Eric's in just as much danger. And if *he* is, then we all are.

What about Papa having to stay in the army all the time? He only comes home on weekends. That's a sign too, isn't it? Sunday night, when he left, he said: "André, you're the man of the house. When I'm away, you're the boss." How could he say such a thing? Doesn't he know what Maman and Cécile are like? He knows very well that they'd never, ever listen to me.

But I don't want to think about that. I'm not that sure that something bad is going to happen. But I do know that the army isn't as safe as all that.

And if there's no war, why do we have those air raid warnings all the time? Maman says it's because the Allies are flying over. The English and the Americans. They're our friends and wouldn't do us any harm. But when I asked why we still had to stay inside, she said, "Just to make sure. In case they make a mistake."

"But can't they *see* where they are?"

"Yes, they can. But they're never really sure. From above everything looks very small. And we're very close to the border here. And on the other side it's war."

So I'd been right all along. There *was* a war after all. On the other side of the border. And we were close to the border. The Germans could come at any moment. Papa had said that himself. The other day I heard him say, "If they want to, the Germans can invade us overnight."

Since the day Papa said that I often see the Ger-

[173]

mans. When I'm in bed, with my pajamas on (so that I can't run away), they come out of the dark. I don't even dare cry for help. There are so many of them, they're so big and they're all over! With their evil faces, their filthy hair, and their sharp claws they look like the wolves in the stories.

Cécile says wolves aren't ugly at all. She's seen them herself, in the zoo in Basel. But she only says that because she doesn't want me to be scared. Because I'm still so little. I didn't want to go to Basel and stayed home with Maman. They let me because my throat was hurting a little anyway.

The station was packed. You'd think the whole world had come to Vevey. They'd decorated the platform with Swiss and French flags. They were even selling ice cream! Maman said she'd buy me one as soon as Jean arrived.

But when was that train going to get here? It was already ten minutes late. Maman said that wasn't very long for a train coming all the way from Lyons. They were very strict at the border because everybody wanted to get into Switzerland. The woman standing next to us said that people tried to hide themselves everywhere. They were even found hanging under the carriages, between the wheels. I didn't want to think of that. But I kept imagining what it would be like. It seemed terribly scary. Especially when the train was going . . . Just think! If you fell, the wheels would run over your hands and your legs. Or over your head. That was even worse, then you'd surely be dead.

The Germans only let children cross the border. And only if they were really starving. If they were, they were allowed to stay with a Swiss family for three months.

There he was. Oh . . . how skinny he was! His hair,

[174]

cut so short you could see his scalp. That wasn't the worst of it. The worst was that he smelled terrible. They all do. Maman said it was because of the powder for head lice. *Yechh!* And *that* had to come and stay in our house!

There was a label around his neck and Maman checked it one last time. It said "Jean Duclos." So it was really him.

Jean doesn't like our food. He doesn't dare to say it, but I can see it when he swallows. Once, when I asked him if he had to finish his porridge at home too, he said that they didn't have porridge in France. Then he bent his head and kept looking at the tablecloth. And after a while I saw tears running down his cheeks.

But Jean is naughty too. He plays with matches all the time. Secretly, of course. We found out when Cécile's doll caught fire. There's nothing left of her hair, just a few wisps! Now he has to stay in my room for three whole days and nights. When I ask him why he did it he won't answer. He just sits on the edge of his bed and stares straight ahead.

Maman is always angry at dinner time. It's all because Jean eats so little. She says he came to us to get big and strong. And if he doesn't eat he'll be just as skinny when he goes home. But now, Maman's asked Jean what he likes the best. And she's cooked it specially for him a few times.

Jean is finally eating normally and he's feeling more at home. You can tell because he takes my bicycle without asking. And he plays with the children next door as if they were *his* friends. I'm glad he's leaving soon. Then I'll have my room to myself again. It's such a mess now. There are far too many things in the closet and his books are always lying on my table.

I like to have houseguests. But not for too long. Jean is used to being here now and he just takes everything for granted. He acts as if all my things were also his. He even does it with Maman. He lets her cuddle him as if he didn't have a mother of his own, at home. Maman has her hands full with Cécile and me.

It was a long trip to the nature preserve in the Jura. The whole class was hungry even before we arrived. When the teacher asked, "Who wants to eat?" we all shouted, "Me!" "Good, then let's eat," she said. "But first let's walk to that spot up there, between the trees."

We ran up to the place and got out our sandwiches. Then the teacher said, "Children! Do you see that stone wall over there?"

"Yes!"

"Well, that's the border."

I couldn't believe it. Were we so near to the border? It couldn't be true, she must be wrong. After all, those few stones there . . . That couldn't be a border, could it? Certainly not the border of a country that was at war. And occupied by the Germans. Wasn't that far too dangerous? If the Germans wanted to, they could step over that little wall, just like that.

"Look," the teacher said, "there is a German soldier over there. Let's go and see him." She got up and pulled me along. What was I to do? I couldn't tell her that I kept seeing Germans at night, could I? And that I had terrible dreams about them? Maybe I could have told her, but not with the others around. They were all following us and they weren't afraid at all. What should I do? I could quietly let go of her hand and stay behind. She wouldn't even notice. The other children were talking to her all the time. But we were getting closer and closer and she was still holding onto my hand. And then suddenly I heard her say something to the German. Oh God! What should I do? I looked back to where we'd come from, as if I'd seen something there. But the

[176]

children shouted, "Come on, André! What is it? Are you scared or something?"

I had to do something. My heart was thumping in my throat. I turned around and saw the German soldier. But he didn't notice and kept on talking to the teacher. That was lucky, I had a chance to get a quick look at him. I did it and he still didn't notice. I looked once more, not as quickly as before. And then I saw that he had normal eyes, nothing special! He had a human face, a nose and two eyes. He was wearing a uniform, just like Papa. Only the color was different. And all of a sudden I thought, *I'm not scared anymore!* The Germans aren't monsters, they're ordinary human beings, just like us.

One night the planes came very close. And it sounded as though they were dropping bombs. We went upstairs and looked out the window in the attic. We saw a lot of light over Renens. It was beautiful and I had to keep telling myself that it wasn't fireworks.

The next morning a whole lot of boys were standing around Pierre in the schoolyard. He said he'd been to Renens. He'd biked there right after the air raid, with his father. They had seen the firemen on ladders. Luckily there hadn't been any dead. A few people had been badly wounded. A woman who had jumped out the window had broken her leg. And a piece of a beam had hit a child on the head. Both had to be taken to the hospital by ambulance.

I was jealous of Pierre. He'd seen all those things after they'd just happened. If we went to look there later, it wouldn't be the same. They wouldn't let you get close to the houses. They might even have put barriers around them.

But I still wanted to go and take a look. You never know. I'd never seen something like that for real. And who knew, maybe there'd still be something left to find. A fragment of a bomb, like the one Pierre got. I was so excited all day. After school we all went to Renens. What an adventure! Was this what war was like? I'd imagined something very different. I thought that it would be really scary. But now that I've seen a bombing I'm not afraid anymore. Not at all. I hope (but of course I won't tell anyone) that it will happen again soon. And this time I'll get there right away.

Today André says:

"I think that one is more afraid of war if one has never experienced it. For me the war has always stayed a menace that never became concrete. It made me more anxious because I could not confront it. So I do not know if you can confront it and still survive. In a sense I am more fragile than those who experienced the war and survived. I realize this when I compare myself to people who have lived through the war. They seem to have more self-confidence, even if they are weaker than I.

"The war can't be as terrible in real life as it is in our imagination, where the worst moments come one right after the other, like they do in films. We shouldn't forget that daily life goes on, families grow closer to each other, and stupid problems lose their importance.

"Until a few years ago I was an overanxious person. Then my best friend got a fatal illness and I nursed him until the end. Today I no longer live in fear of the disasters that life has in store for me. Confronting the worst has probably made me stronger."

André is a journalist. He lives and works in Lausanne.

BIRTHE

DENMARK

Far* always sends me to bed at seven o'clock, when I'm not at all sleepy. He tells me I can still read a little, but I don't feel like that at all. I prefer to look out the window, at the children playing outside. Jytte is always with them. She too is only five years old, but she's allowed to stay up till eight.

Jytte often goes on outings on the bicycle with her father. Far doesn't even have a children's seat on his. But that doesn't matter, I can sit on the bar in front. Only he's never gotten around to taking me along because he's always much too busy.

Far is always on the phone in the evening. I once asked Mor** if that was because of his job. But she said, "No. He is busy with other things." That's what I thought too, because his voice sounds so different. He is always getting angry and talks about those "dirty pigs" and says, "Just wait and see. We'll get them in the end." When I hear him talk like that I always have to shudder.

*"Father" in Danish.
**"Mother" in Danish.

And I pull the blanket up over my ears so that I don't have to listen.

Mor says that I'm much too curious. I can't help it, I keep having to think of that cupboard. The chocolates and Mor's cigarettes are in there. Far is the only one who has the key. Oh, how I'd like to look in that cupboard—just for a second. I'm sure I wouldn't care so much anymore once I knew what's in there.

I'll just go and take a peek! I'll do it now! Far is taking his nap anyway. He always does that after lunch. And his bunch of keys is lying next to him on the table. I've taken the keys. . . . He hasn't noticed anything. . . . I am tiptoeing to the cupboard now. . . . What if he suddenly wakes up? What do I do then?

He never wakes up all at once. First he stops snoring. And I can hear that from here, in the other room. I'll just have to listen very carefully. And if it gets quiet all of a sudden, I'll quickly put the keys back.

The lock opens easily. . . . I leave the door ajar a little bit. Then you can't hear it creak.

Oh . . . Look! What's that? What are those things doing here in the cupboard? And where have they come from? They don't belong to Far, do they?

My goodness! A soldier's cap! It looks like a real one. . . . The ones the Germans wear look exactly like this. And that band for around the arm . . . with that big swastika. And a stick that they use to hit people with. And also photos of men in uniform. What are those things doing *here?*

Oh . . . There's also a pistol. It couldn't be a real one, could it?

How heavy it is. I pick it up, just like that. Without thinking. Careful, Birthe! Hold it tight . . . it could slip out of your hand. How come my hands are so wet all of a sudden?

Since I looked in the cupboard I feel so mixed up inside. Everything is a big jumble in there.

I wish I'd never opened that cupboard. Then I wouldn't know what's in it. So I keep telling myself that I only *planned* to, but that in the end I didn't really do it. Sometimes I believe myself for a little while. But then suddenly I'm sure again that I did. So I just try not to think about it. But that doesn't always work. Especially not when it's dark and I'm lying in my bed.

If only I could tell somebody about it. But if I tell Mor she'll scold me, of course. And who knows, she might even tell Far.

I don't dare tell Jytte either. Because what would she think? She might even believe that Far is doing bad things. And that's not true at all. My Far doesn't do bad things. What he does is always good. Even if it's a secret.

Before, I always wanted to know all secrets. But now I know that secrets are not at all always nice.

Mrs. Christensen from downstairs is talking with Mor. Something terrible has happened. I can hear that.

This morning, when I came into the kitchen, Mor sat there crying. I knew right away that it was something to do with Far. She said that he'd gone to Copenhagen. But if that were true she wouldn't be so sad, because Far goes to Copenhagen often enough.

Poor Mor. . . . I'd love to help her. But I can't. The only thing I can do is to be a good girl. And not whine. That's why I stopped asking where Far is.

"I hear cars," says Mrs. Christensen, and she goes over to the window. Mrs. Christensen has had such a shock that her voice is hoarse as she says: "Two officers. They're coming in this direction. I'll just quickly go back downstairs."

I hear them coming up the stairs. That noise of their boots on the linoleum. They're nearly upstairs. In

[183]

a minute they'll be at the door. And then they'll click their heels . . .

Oh! I wish I wasn't here! That I could disappear. Or hide. But I can't even move. I'm all stiff and my legs feel like cotton wool.

How brave Mor is. When they ring the bell she goes to the door and opens it. One of the Germans says, "Hello, Mrs. Knudsen. *Heil Hitler!* Forgive us for disturbing you."

How polite he is. I'd never have thought it. Maybe they won't do us any harm. Who knows, maybe they are very kind. And maybe they've just come to tell us that Far will be coming home soon. Why not? Why didn't I think of that before?

"Can you tell me where my husband is?" Mor is asking.

"He is with us, at the Gestapo. But he'll be going to Kolding soon."

"And when can I see him?"

"Not right now. You'll have to have a little patience, Mrs. Knudsen."

He nods to the other officer. This one takes a step forward and puts Far's wallet, watch, and keys on the table. Then he says to Mor, "We just came to bring you your husband's personal possessions. And to ask if there is anything we can do for you."

Mor asks: "Can I send him a few things? His shaving gear and his toothbrush?"

"Don't worry about that, Mrs. Knudsen. He can get those from us. If we think he needs them."

"So all I can do is wait."

"I'm afraid so, Mrs. Knudsen."

It looks as if Mor is going to cry. But she stays brave. The German now says, "Oh, yes . . . I nearly forgot. Your husband asked me to tell you that your cigarettes are in the cupboard."

When they've left, Mor immediately calls Grandpa

[184]

and Grandma to tell them that Far is being sent to the prison at Kolding.

I wish I still was a tiny little baby, like Svend. He's been fast asleep all morning and hasn't noticed that anything's been going on.

Grandpa stops by every night to tuck us in. Sometimes, if he's in a good mood, he tells a little story. But when he found out that I had gone to the Aabenraa Road he got a little angry. He said that I'm much too curious, and since then he calls me a nosy little girl.

When I heard that there had been an attack in the Aabenraa Road I ran there immediately. I saw the soldiers and the horses just lying there in the middle of the road. The soldiers had at least been covered with blankets. But the horses . . . I still shiver to think of it. Those poor horses . . . I still see them before me, with their round bellies and their long thin legs. They were so sad, but also a little creepy. Those big bulging eyes seemed to be looking at me.

"Mor! Come here! Quick!"

She was already there and asked, "What's the matter with you, Birthe? You're all wet and your teeth are chattering."

"I had such a terrible dream! I dreamt that they were after me. Just like Erik . . ."

"Now where did you hear that story?"

"Jytte told me."

Suddenly I had to cry and I told her everything. That Jytte came to fetch me when she'd heard her mother talking on the phone. Her mother had been called by a friend who knew that Erik was dead. That friend had seen the Germans chasing him herself and she had also heard them firing as he climbed over a wall.

Jytte wanted me to go with her to the place where

it had happened. But I said no because I knew it wasn't allowed. "Come on," she said. "Nobody has to find out. It's not far from here and we'll soon be back."

When we got there there was nothing to see. We thought the story couldn't be true. But suddenly I saw a few red spots on the cobblestones. I realized it was blood. . . . Blood from Erik. . . . That had been his . . . Blood that had been inside him. . . . Not so long ago, maybe only an hour. . . .

And when I realized that just one hour ago Erik was still running, and climbing over a wall, and *alive,* I got so sick that I had to throw up.

"You see now, Birthe. That's what happens when you want to see everything."

"But I didn't want to at all! It was Jytte."

"It was very stupid of Jytte too. But you still went with her."

"I'll never, ever do it again, Mor! I promise!"

She gave me a kiss and said, "Now just go back to sleep."

Sleep? How could I go to sleep now? I was so scared. "Please . . . Don't leave me alone."

"What are you afraid of, my darling?"

"I'm so afraid for Far. That he—just like Erik . . ."

"Come on, Birthe. You shouldn't be thinking of things like that. Far is in Kolding. You know that, don't you?"

"But he's been there forever. And we never hear a thing."

"That's because they don't allow him to write. But they promised me that he'll be coming home."

"But *when?*"

"I don't know. I hope very son."

"You mean before Christmas?"

"I really hope so, sweetheart. But I can't promise."

[186]

At Christmas the family is always together. Either we go to Padborg or they come to Haderslev. This year Aunt Mette and Lars and Olaf are coming here. Without Uncle Jesper because he's still in Germany, in a camp.

I'm glad I saved all my pocket money. Now I can buy presents for everybody. This time I'm going to buy the nicest presents for Far and Uncle Jesper.

We still haven't had any news. Not from Far and not from Uncle Jesper either. But they will come for Christmas, I'm sure about that. The Germans are mean, but they can't be that mean. They'll let them go home, even if it's just for a few days. It will be terrible if they have to go back afterwards. But it will still be better than nothing at all. Then at least we'll have been together for a little while.

Aunt Mette and the boys have gone this morning back to Padborg. I had hidden Far's and Uncle Jesper's presents behind the couch, in case they showed up at the very last moment. But now I have to find another place for them.

They've called to say that Far is coming home. Oh, I'm so excited! I'm so happy. I've never been so happy in my life. At last I too have a Far again. Just like all the other children.

Mor says that we have to be very quiet in the beginning. We mustn't make any noise and walk on our tiptoes. But I don't mind that at all. I'll do anything for my darling Far.

The doorbell is ringing. That must be him. . . . Quick, quick, run to the door. . . . Oh, how far away it seems. How long it's taking to get there. . . .

When Mor opens the door I don't dare look right away. I hide behind her. And Svend keeps pulling at my skirt. He doesn't understand what is going on. He doesn't even remember Far anymore.

Far is standing with his arms around Mor. I hear her cry. But it's not from sadness. It's because she's so happy.

Now I finally dare to look . . . But is that Far? That skinny, gray man? Nobody told me that he's been sick! Far is sitting on the couch and Mor asks me to get the tea. I tiptoe to the kitchen and return with the big tray. Far says that he isn't thirsty right now. "A cookie?" I ask. "No, maybe later . . ."

And then suddenly, as we are having our tea, Far asks, "What is that rattling sound I keep hearing?" I don't know what he means, but Mor says, "Birthe, stop stirring your cup for a moment."

Svend is staying with Grandma and Grandpa because it was much too busy for Far. And I'm at Jytte's nearly all the time. Her mother doesn't mind, luckily. She says: "You have to be patient. It will pass. It's only been five weeks since he came home. . . ."

Sometimes I think that Far will never again be the way he was before. He doesn't do a thing all day. He just sits there in his chair and stares out the window.

The only time I really see Far is at the table when we're eating. And then he keeps hiding his hands. I've told myself a million times that I don't have to look at them. Two of his fingers don't have nails anymore. I know that they have pulled them out in jail. But he shouldn't find out that I know that.

But I would like to see them—just once. Then at least I'd know how they looked. And I'm sure that then it wouldn't be so difficult to pretend I don't notice.

I hate the Germans. Oh, how I hate them! When I think about them I just get the goose bumps. It's their fault that Far has changed so much and that we still haven't heard from Uncle Jesper.

On Liberation Day I stole three eggs from the cellar and took them to the big square. I smashed them right into the faces of those bitches whose heads had been shaved. At last they were getting what was coming to them! I didn't know what they had done exactly, but it was something to do with the Germans. So it had to be something very, very bad.

"Birthe, please. Try to control yourself," says Mor. I've laid my head in her lap but it doesn't stop. We're nearly in Padborg and I'm still howling. I sob, "I'm trying . . . I'm really doing my best . . . but I just can't . . ." "Come on, my little girl . . . I understand," says Mor. Mor understands. Of course she understands. Uncle Jesper was her own brother, after all.

When Aunt Mette called to tell us that the people of the Red Cross had found his body she also cried. They had recognized him because of his front teeth. They had a big gap between them. I remember that very well. I wish they hadn't recognized Uncle Jesper. At least then we could go on hoping. Then we could believe that he might still come back. But now it's certain, completely certain, that we'll never, ever, see him again.

It's all the fault of those rotten Germans. I'll never forgive them for killing Uncle Jesper. My big, strong Uncle Jesper! He loved Aunt Mette so much, he loved Olaf so much, he loved Lars so much. And me, as if I were his own daughter.

Today Birthe says:

"Although I know that there is now a new generation, I still feel a shiver when I think of the Germans. That's why I probably never wanted to think of those times. Before being asked about my memories, I did not even know that I remembered so much. When I read my story it was as if another part of me had opened up. My son asked me, 'Why didn't you ever tell me this?' He actually never knew that his grandfather had been in the Resistance. And now he is very proud of it.

"I think that the experience of the war has made me more human, and I do not mind having gone through it. But I realize that my mother was a very strong woman who did not make a big deal out of anything. Today I am just glad that I did not have to go through it with my own children."

Birthe lives with her husband and two sons in Connecticut.

ZSUZSA

HUNGARY

I was glad Fräulein was holding my hand when we came out of the church. Suddenly there was so much light that it hurt my eyes. It had been so dark in there. And now we were outside again. It had all gone so fast. The priest had said so much. I'd hardly understood any of it.

"Fräulein?"

"Yes, Zsuzsa."

"Am I a Catholic now?"

"Yes. Now you are Catholic."

"Is that what it is, to be baptized?"

"Yes, that's it."

"But don't they do it with water?"

"Yes, with Holy Water."

"Those few little drops. Was that Holy Water?"

"Yes, that's what it was."

"Fräulein?"

"Yes, Zsuzsa."

"If you are a Catholic, then aren't you a Christian too?"

"Yes, of course."

"So then when you're a Christian, then you're also a Catholic."

"No, that's not necessarily so."

"But why not?"

"That's much too complicated to explain. Why do you always have to know everything? Look, let me show you something. I have a surprise for you."

She gave me a little square box. It was tied with a red bow.

"Is that for me?"

"Yes, for you. From your darling mother. I was to give it to you after the ceremony."

It made me go hot all over. What could be inside that little box? I wanted to know so much. But what a pity, to have to ruin that beautiful bow.

"Oh! A little cross! On a chain! How lovely!"

"Let me see how it looks on you. It's beautiful! And the chain is just the right length."

"Is it real gold?"

"Yes. Just look at the box. It's from Bálint. At Bálint they only sell real jewelry."

"How sweet of Anyu* to surprise me! Couldn't we go by the workshop for a minute? I'd like to thank her."

"No, Zsuzsa. You know very well that you mustn't disturb her."

"Yes, Fräulein, I know that. . . ."

What a lovely little cross. I am going to wear it every day. All my life. And the chain is also so beautiful. Very thin, they go so well together. Anyu really knows how to pick these things out. She has such good taste. That's also why she is a dressmaker.

Why doesn't Anyu ever wear a little cross? She is a Catholic too, isn't she? I'm sure of it. So one person

*"Mother" in Hungarian.

wears a cross and the other doesn't. It's one's own choice. Grandma Gizi wears a cross and so do Aunt Teréz and Aunt Margit. They also go to church a lot. Grandma Gizi nearly every day, but Anyu never. Anyu and Apu* didn't even get married in the church. Otherwise I would have seen photographs of that. Everybody has photographs of that, even poor people. I once asked Fräulein why Anyu and Apu didn't have pictures of their wedding. And then I had to promise her that I would never, ever ask that question again.

I think that you can only wear a cross when you've been baptized, when you're a Catholic. That's what people decided, so you could tell who's Catholic and who isn't. But of course you also wear it because it's so pretty.

Aunt Ilonka also used to wear a gold chain like this. Not with a little cross but with a little star. One time I wanted to see how it would look on me, and she let me wear it for a little while. But I haven't seen her wear that little star for quite some time. I hope she hasn't lost it.

"Fräulein?"

"Yes, Zsuzsa. What's the matter?"

Anyu's workshop is in the Váci street; we passed very close to it on our way. Once, when Fräulein had gone to her uncle's funeral, Anyu came to fetch me from school herself. And afterwards she let me come back with her to the workshop. One of the seamstresses gave me a magnet that she used to pick up pins. You could pick up at least a thousand pins in one go with it. And you could make lots of nice things with that clump of pins. Another seamstress let me play with the bobbins of thread. First I put the nicest colors next to each other: red, blue, and yellow. And after that I sorted them into

*"Father" in Hungarian.

groups of each color and placed them next to each other in a row going from light to dark.

It is so nice and cozy in the workshop. Anyu is often busy with the clients, but I don't mind at all. I know that she is close by, in the salon. And when everybody has left I am allowed to sit for a moment on the elegant chairs in the salon. They are so beautiful! The wood is all gold and the cushions are made of pink silk.

Anyu is such a darling, she really wouldn't mind if we dropped in for a moment now, I thought. So I said: "Can't we . . . Just for a bit. . . ."

"Stop it, Zsuzsa! If you keep whining like that I'll have no more surprises for you!"

"What?" Another surprise?

"Yes. You're really being incredibly spoiled."

"What? Tell me, what?"

"You can have an ice cream on the terrace at Gerbaud's."

"Oh, how wonderful! I'd like mocha, please."

"See, how sweet your mother is! She even treats you to an ice cream. And at Gerbaud's, of all places. There aren't many girls of seven who can say they have eaten ice cream at Gerbaud's."

I knew very well that Anyu was spoiling me. It was already the third time she'd let me have an ice cream there. And the ice cream at Gerbaud's is so good. If you take mocha there's even a piece of chocolate on the top.

Tomorrow I'll tell Vera that I've been to Gerbaud's. Will she be jealous, I wonder? No, that isn't her way. But if she's never been there herself, she might not be too happy about it. Better not to say anything then. What a pity. It would be so nice to tell her about it. And it would be even nicer to eat an ice cream together on the terrace. At Gerbaud's there are so few children. At least I've never seen one there yet.

At Miss Tauber's it normally took a very long time before she opened the door. The room where she taught was at the very end of the corridor. And she also walked so slowly because there was something wrong with her leg.

When Fräulein rung the bell I thought, *Now I'm going to do it!* I'll rush down the stairs, into the street, and run to the Danube. To the spot where the stone steps go all the way down into the water. There I'll sit, take off my shoes, and dip my feet in the water!

But I waited just a little too long. Just as I was about to turn around I heard Miss Tauber switch on the light in the hall.

Fräulein took off my coat and stayed in the front room, reading a magazine. I always went ahead of Miss Tauber. That way it looked as if I was in a hurry to get to the piano. But that wasn't it at all. I only did it because then I didn't have to see how she dragged her foot.

When I was sitting on the piano bench Miss Tauber asked, "Did you practice well?"

Since she asked me that each time, I always had the same answer, "Yes, Miss Tauber. I did my best. But it was a little difficult."

And then she said, just as always, "All right then, let's hear what you have learned this week."

But just as I was about to begin, she suddenly said in a very different voice, "My dear child . . . I see that they've had you baptized. How smart of your parents."

She sighed deeply, and I quickly started to play. I'd just begun when the bell rang. Great! Now I could stop! And the lesson would be shorter, she couldn't keep me there longer than usual. I knew that at four another girl was coming.

How nice, Miss Tauber was staying away a long time. Suddenly Fräulein came into the room. Her voice was all hoarse and she said, "They have come to fetch Miss Tauber. And we have to go with her."

There were three men in dark uniforms. They looked like policemen. They had bands with swastikas on their arms. They were very severe and said that they had very little time. We had to hurry and walk quickly to the car. When they noticed how Miss Tauber dragged her foot they were very mean. They laughed and said that they would soon teach her to walk faster. And she really was doing her very best!

When I saw her like that I was sorry that I'd always been such a nuisance to her. It wasn't her fault that I disliked playing the piano so much, was it?

At the police station Fräulein got very angry. She said it was a scandal. We had no business being there. And that I was only a little child. What did they want from us? We had to go home at once. Then they changed their tune and said very politely, "All right, we will take the child home. But you must stay a little longer."

The policeman rang the doorbell and Anyu opened the door. She gave me a big kiss and I saw right away that she'd been very worried. Apu was also home, and Aunt Bözsi and Aunt Ilonka were also there. I was so happy because I hadn't seen Apu for so long. When he came home in the evenings I was already in bed, and on Sundays they always went to visit friends.

But I soon found out that they weren't there for the fun of it. They were worried and wanted to know exactly what had happened. I tried to tell it as well as I could because I noticed that they thought it was very important. And when they'd asked me everything so often that I kept giving the same answers, they started talking among themselves. Very quietly, so that I couldn't hear.

I did so want to know why the police had taken Miss Tauber. But nobody told me anything. Was it a secret that I didn't have the right to know? Or did they think that I already knew it?

The next day was washing day and then I could ask Juci, I thought. Fräulein and the maid laughed at Juci because she was so fat and stupid. But I loved her and I didn't mind at all that she was fat. She was very nice and I could discuss everything with her. And I didn't think she was stupid. Once, when I asked her if it was really true that there was a war on, she'd said, "Yes, it's been on for three years, already." And when I wanted to know why you could hardly notice there was a war on, she said: "Lucky for us, the Germans have left us alone so far."

I didn't exactly understand what she meant then, but at least now I knew for sure that there was a war on. Every time I asked Fräulein the same question, she'd start to laugh or she'd talk about something else completely.

Anyu was at the workshop, Fräulein was talking to her friend on the telephone, and the maid was making the beds. I sneaked to the scullery, where Juci stood before the washtub.

"Juci! I was at the police station yesterday!"

"Hey, what's that you're telling me now, my darling Zsuzsa? That's no place for little girls like you!"

"I was at my piano lesson and then they came to fetch us. The teacher, Fräulein, and me. But they let me go right away. And Fräulein came back last night at ten o'clock."

"And your teacher?"

"I don't know. I think she is still there. Anyu tried to call her. But there is no answer."

"What a crying shame! You hear so many things lately."

"Juci? Do you know why they came to get her?"

[197]

"Of course not, my darling. How would I know that? I don't know your teacher, do I?"

"Her name is Tauber. I thought maybe you also worked at her place."

"No. And the name doesn't mean anything to me. Is she Jewish?"

I didn't know what that was. But I had heard the word often. Always very softly and quickly whispered. As if it was something shameful. A kind of disease that you had to keep secret.

I said, "I don't know. How can you tell? Does it show?"

"Not really. . . . Well, maybe a little. . . . Most Jews have dark hair and big noses. They're good at learning and they're all rich."

When Juci said that I saw Miss Tauber before me. She had black frizzy hair and a crooked nose. And suddenly I remembered how she had sighed when she saw my little golden cross. I knew then for sure that she was Jewish.

The seamstresses now work here at home in the guest room and I'm allowed in there all the time. Aunt Bözsi and Aunt Ilonka are living in the Váci Street workshop and I go there every day with Fräulein. On our way there we buy food because they themselves never go out. Nobody is allowed to know that they live there now.

Once, when we were there, the caretaker rang the doorbell. Aunt Bözsi and Aunt Ilonka suddenly turned all white. Aunt Ilonka ran as fast as she could to the WC and Aunt Bözsi dove into the wardrobe, where Anyu's designs used to hang. Aunt Bözsi in the wardrobe! I'd never have thought it possible! She was much too round and much too fat! It was so funny to see those two fat

[198]

aunts playing hide and seek. But I couldn't even laugh.
I had to sit still and be quiet.

Luckily the caretaker didn't notice anything. But
Aunt Ilonka and Aunt Bözsi had a terrible fright. When
we left they were still shaking.

Apu is going away. He has to go on a trip. I don't
know where and I don't know how long he'll stay away
either. He doesn't feel like going at all and I'm afraid
that he isn't going to have a good time there.

He has to leave in six days' time. Anyu is working
with the seamstresses to get his things ready. I have a
bag full of patches and I have picked out the nicest ones.
They look so nice together, so I'm going to make a little
cushion out of them. It's a big job and I've already been
working on it for three days. One of the seamstresses
said that she wouldn't mind helping me. But I don't
want that, I want to do it myself, otherwise it's not
really mine. Apu has to take something that's all mine.

I don't know exactly what he is going to use my
little cushion for over there. But you can do all sorts of
things with it. It can keep you warm and is so nice and
soft. Apu can only take very few things with him, just a
rucksack. Luckily my little cushion will just fit.

I'm sure that Apu is going to miss me a lot when
he's so far away. But then he'll suddenly remember that
he has my little cushion. And then, when he touches it,
he won't feel so lonely anymore.

We're allowed to take Apu to the train station. I am
wearing my new coat for the first time. It is light blue
and the collar and the buttons are made of navy velvet.

I am so happy that Apu can see me like this. In my
new coat I don't look like such a little girl anymore but
almost like a real young lady.

Apu is walking between Anyu and me. He hardly

says a thing and he looks very pale. But he is holding my hand firmly. I look at the other children who are walking next to their fathers. Some of them are crying and want to be carried.

We have to walk quite far because the train is terribly long. There are at least a hundred wagons and it's taking a long time for us to get to the one Apu has to go in.

I'm sure something is going to happen soon. At the last moment, when I'm saying good-bye to Apu.

There are German soldiers on the platform, some of them with big police dogs. They see me walking in my beautiful coat next to Apu. At Apu's wagon there will be a soldier too. And I'm sure that just as Apu is bending down to kiss me, he will say, "Sir, you don't have to leave. You have such a sweet little daughter. It would be a shame to leave her behind."

But it doesn't go that way at all. When Apu kisses me, nothing like that happens. He is pushed along with many other men into the carriage and can't even wave good-bye. And the German soldiers who have been looking on so quietly suddenly start shouting very loudly.

On the way home I feel terribly cold, and when I come home I have a high fever. Anyu puts me to bed at once and I must stay indoors for a whole week.

Fräulein says that it is a miracle that Anyu was able to leave the town. The heavy bombing started the day she left. The Russians are already very close and the Germans just don't want to leave. That's why we're living in the cellar now and have been for I don't know how long.

Every time the noise of the bombing gets louder, Fräulein starts to tremble. Then she goes all white and she gets so cold that I can hear her teeth chattering.

Fräulein is the only one I have left, the only one

[200]

who has stayed with me. I love her very much. I only wish she wouldn't be so afraid, I hate that. Sometimes I'm a little scared myself, but I can't tell her because I know that she herself is much more afraid. It wouldn't help anyway, because she is afraid of different things—like bombs. I don't really worry so much about them. Because you can see the bombs, you can hear them, and they are there for everyone. If they hit you it's just bad luck.

I am afraid of things that are much more scary. Of the real dangers—the ones you can't see. I am so afraid that something will happen to Anyu. She just left, just like that, all by herself, to look for Apu. And she doesn't even know where he is because we still haven't heard from him.

The best place to be is on my mattress under my quilt. And then I watch the shadows on the walls. It's like a strange puppet show with witches and fairies. Even though it's only the people around me, moving around in the candlelight.

But what I like most is to lie here with my eyes shut. Then the only things I see are big white clouds. And then a white horse and a white carriage come driving up over the clouds. A handsome young prince and a princess with long blond hair are sitting on the driver's box. When they come closer I see that they are not a prince and a princess at all, but my own Apu and my own Anyu. They drive on and on, they are flying high above me, way up in the air. I don't think they can see me, lying here in the cellar on my mattress. But then I feel myself lifted up very gently. And before I know it, I am sitting between them and together we fly above the white clouds in the blue sky.

What a bang! Everything is shaking! Everyone is screaming. There's no light. Somebody is shouting:

[201]

"Quick! Quick! The emergency exit!" I hear a few muffled bangs, and then I see lots of bright light shining through a narrow crack. Everybody is relieved and people are beginning to push toward the exit. They are pushing so hard that I can hardly stay on my feet. But they're cheerful and keep saying, "How lucky we are! If the emergency exit had been buried, we would all have suffocated to death in here!"

Suddenly I hear somebody call, "Zsuzsa, Zsuzsa! Where are you?"

The voice is coming from the outside and I shout back as loud as I can, "Here! Down here, in the cellar!"

"Zsuzsa! Please . . . Answer me! It's me, your Aunt Teréz!"

"Yes! I am right here! In the cellar!"

Thank goodness, she has heard me. She asks, "You aren't hurt, are you?"

"No, not at all. I am all right!"

"What's keeping you? Why don't you come out?"

"There are a lot of people ahead of me."

"And what about Fräulein?"

"She is here too."

When I climb out we wait for Fräulein. Only she doesn't come and everybody else is already out.

Aunt Teréz shouts, "Fräulein! Come on now! Hurry up!"

"I'm coming!"

"What's the matter? You're not hurt, are you?"

"No, but I can't find it . . ."

"Can't find what?"

"The pan?"

"What pan?"

"The little pan with the food."

"Leave it! Who cares about that little pan?!"

"But there was still a bit of goulash left!"

"Come on, hurry up, will you! Forget the goulash! Everything could collapse any time now!"

"I've found it! I'm coming!"

The first thing we see coming out is the little pan. It is all covered with dust and the lid is only half on. That Fräulein . . . She's done nothing but tremble and shake. And now a bomb has fallen on our house, she only thinks about the leftovers in the pan.

When Grandma Gizi saw me she cried, "Come here, come here, my poor child! That mother of yours, she has abandoned you. And all because of that Jew. . . ."

Suddenly I understood everything. That Apu was Jewish. That was why they had deported him.

What a shame that Grandma Gizi did not like the Jews. I heard that clearly in her voice. But she said it so honestly. At least now I know why Anyu's family is so different from Apu's.

I have been here only a few days but already I feel completely at home. We often sit all together around the table, sorting lentils. And then we tell each other all kinds of stories. I didn't use to like lentils. But Grandma Gizi knows how to cook them in at least a hundred different ways. That's just as well, because there isn't anything else to eat anyway.

I am not such a baby anymore as when I was with Fräulein. The first day, Grandma Gizi gave me a little bowl with water and a towel and now I wash myself every day. I can also brush my own hair now, and I can nearly braid it all by myself too.

There is a mirror hanging on a nail in the wall. That's where Aunt Teréz and Aunt Margit stand when they put on their makeup. They don't mind if I watch them while they're doing it. It's such fun to watch, they do it so fast and so neatly. They look exactly like Anyu,

[203]

with their blue eyes and blond hair. Sometimes I also stand before the mirror to have a look at myself. What will I look like later? I won't be as beautiful as Anyu, that's for sure, because I don't have blond hair and blue eyes. With my curly brown hair and my green eyes I look much more like Apu, I suppose.

Uncle Laci says that the siege really cannot last much longer because the Russians are coming a little closer every day. In a few days, a week at most, we'll be liberated. Uncle Laci should know, because he sometimes goes outside. It's very dangerous, but he does it anyway.

I don't even remember how life was before the bombings. It's going to be strange not to live in a cellar anymore. And to see such a big difference between day and night.

Yesterday, when nobody was looking, I sneaked out of the cellar. I walked into the street, to the shop that had been bombed and where Uncle Laci had found two huge crystal vases. He had said that there were still lots of other things lying around. But when I arrived the shop was completely empty.

It started to snow. I didn't feel like going back at all. It was lovely in the street. I hadn't been outside for so long!

There was nobody around. But suddenly I saw a few people in the distance. They were smashing open a shop window that had been only a little damaged. I just wanted to take a look. And when I came nearer I saw that it was a toy shop!

If I took something now . . . was that stealing? Yes, of course it was. But weren't they all doing it? So then it must be all right after all. If a shop was destroyed by a bomb then you could take things.

I didn't know where to look first. There were two big, long boxes lying on the counter. I lifted the cover of one of them and there was a doll with real hair and porcelain blue eyes! I quickly grabbed both boxes and ran home with them.

They're all mine, they belong to me. I rescued them myself from the bombs. In my little room at home I had twenty-seven dolls. They are all gone now. How lucky I was to find these! I already love them so much that I wouldn't exchange them for all the others.

What shall I call them? Such beautiful dolls have to have a very special name. Strange, suddenly I can't think of any. Am I such a bad doll's mother, then? I need two names and I can't think of one! Don't worry darlings—if I hold you both in my arms long enough, it will surely come to me.

Which one do I think is sweeter? Which one do I love more? It's difficult to say because they're exactly the same. They even have the same dress: light blue trimmed with white lace. The only difference is that one of them is a little bit damaged, she has a little spot on her left cheek.

Katika, the daughter of the caretaker, is always right behind me when I'm playing with my dolls. She keeps asking me where I found them and if there are any more. I know! I'll give her one of them! They are exactly the same anyway and I only need one. *Veronka!* That's a beautiful name! Suddenly I've found it. Without even thinking, it came to me, just like that. And I am very sure of it. That name, no other name, is the one that suits her. "Katika . . . Look . . . I'll give you this one."

She gets very shy and says: "Really, you mean it?"

"Yes. Here, take it."

"But I can't. I have no right, just like that . . ."

[205]

"Why not? They are both mine. I found them myself."

She takes the doll I give her and says:

"Hey, you're giving me the wrong one."

"What do you mean?"

"You gave me the one that is undamaged."

My sweet little Veronka. You are a bit wounded. But I'll make you all better and that spot on your face will soon heal. And if in the end there's still a scar, I won't mind at all. I'll love you just as much, maybe even more. The other doll is a tiny bit more beautiful . . . But I could never give you, my dear Veronka, away.

The Russians have come. It has been four weeks already. We are now living upstairs again and everybody is happy that we are finally free.

Nobody talks about Anyu. Grandma Gizi thinks that she is dead. Of course she doesn't say that, but I know what she thinks. The other day, when the door was ajar, I heard Aunt Teréz say, "I really can't keep her. . . . What am I to do with a child of ten?"

I ran into the garden and flung myself face down in the snow. I lay there like that for a very long time. In the end I got so cold that I stopped thinking completely. I may even have fallen asleep. Because I know that suddenly I remembered everything again. And I thought, *Please no, I don't want to get up anymore.* But then I realized I was all wet and so I got up anyway.

Anyu is back! My dear Anyu! I am so happy! I am so happy! I have never been so happy in all my life!

She came on foot, all the way from Sopron through the deep snow, with only one piece of bread to eat. And when she was finally home she saw that our building had been destroyed. She had a terrible shock because she was sure I was buried under the rubble! With her last remaining strength she ran to Grandma Gizi's house and when she saw me here she collapsed.

When Anyu talks about her search for Apu she starts to cry. First she went to Aunt Magda, because Uncle Géza is a lieutenant and he was working in the concentration camp Sopron Köhida. But they weren't nice to her at all. They let her sleep on the couch but they kept it a secret. And they didn't want to help her either. Uncle Géza only said that Apu was not in his camp. And when she begged to ask about him at the other camps, he said that he couldn't do that. So then she went all by herself from one camp to the other but they never let her in. The only thing she could do was look at the prisoners behind the barbed wire. But they all looked alike because they were all bald and wore the same kind of clothes. Everywhere she went she'd shout Apu's name, but the prisoners were too far away to hear her.

I was at the station once when a transport arrived. The way they looked! Just like skeletons! They looked as if they don't even know where they were.

But when they passed close to us, my heart started to beat faster and faster. Suddenly I was sure that Apu was among them. He must be—surely he was one of these men, only we didn't recognize him!

But after a while the platform was empty. Everybody had left. Anyu said that he would have seen us even if we had not recognized him.

Whenever we go to the train station we carry a big sign that says, *"Stark Miklós, thirty-seven years old. Has anyone seen him?"* Once somebody stopped and said that he had slept in the same barracks as a man called Stark Miklós. But when they were freed Stark Miklós was so weak he stayed behind on his wooden bed. The last thing he'd heard was that they had taken Stark Miklós to the hospital.

On our way home I asked Anyu: "Do you think that Apu is still alive?"

"I don't know, my sweetheart . . ."

"But he was still alive when they freed him! Once the war is over, you don't die, do you?"

"Most of the time, no. But sometimes, yes. Some people are so weak and exhausted that nothing can be done for them anymore."

"How horrible! But how could such a dreadful thing happen to him, of all people?"

"So many horrible things can happen. But we have to keep hoping."

We passed a cemetery and Anyu said that she felt like praying. I sat down to wait on a little bench while she prayed. When she'd finished she came and sat down next to me. It was very quiet and I didn't really know what to say to her. So I just said, "It's beautiful here." And then she said, "Yes, but life is not beautiful!" and she burst into tears. She cried so hard that her whole body shook. I so much wanted to comfort her but I knew that I couldn't. If only I could cry too, at least we'd be doing it together. But I couldn't cry, even though I wanted to very much, because I felt all dried up inside.

It's been two years since I've been in school here with the nuns. Anyu can't have me because she's working in the factory from early in the morning until late at night. If only Apu would come back, then everything would be back to normal!

Anyu says that it is not good to go on believing that he is still alive. Still, sometimes I'm all but certain that he is somewhere, that he still exists. He could still be too weak to travel, couldn't he? Or, who knows, maybe he's forgotten everything?

[208]

These days some people don't even remember their own name. I heard about a man who had forgotten that he had a wife and children. He was living in Germany and he had married again. But one day, as much as ten years later, he found the house key of his former home in his pocket. And suddenly he remembered everything!

One of the girls asked me why I never talk about my father. I couldn't tell her I believe that he is alive, somewhere. And the story about the hospital is none of her business. It's such a horrible thought that he could have died of exhaustion. Think of it—after the liberation, no less! Anyhow, that story might not be true at all. That's why I simply said, "My father died during the war." She looked at me as if she was about to ask more questions. So I said quickly, "He was a soldier."

That was not a complete lie, because when Apu was young he had been in the army.

Today Zsuzsa says:

"*I still don't know the exact circumstances of my father's death. A few years ago I happened to meet somebody who was there when he died. When I asked him for details he said that he would tell me another time. But strangely enough I never asked him again. Maybe because I do not want to see the version with which I finally have come to terms revised.*

"*Looking back to those childhood years during the war, my biggest problem was that everything was kept secret. Nobody told me that my father was Jewish; I didn't even know what being Jewish meant. All I understood was that it was something shameful. When I found out that my father was Jewish I could not accept it. For many years I denied my Jewish origins and later I was ashamed of having denied it. It was only by marrying a Jew and having Jewish friends that I solved the problem.*

"*The war has left me with a certain distrust of human beings, especially when I suspect them of harboring racist feelings. Another thing that stayed with me is that I am not afraid of dying. Probably having been close to it so often makes death seem a very normal thing.*"

Zsuzsa lives in Geneva, Switzerland, with her husband. She has two married daughters. She works part-time as a laboratory technician.

[210]